RAMONA THE RAINMAKER.
Luster Glazed Porcelain Sculpture. Randall Schmidt.

PILGRIM BOTTLE. Thomas Shafer.

Vase with Enamel.
Polly Rothenberg.

Raku Mural. Paul Rayar.

THE COMPLETE BOOK OF
CERAMIC ART

by POLLY ROTHENBERG

CROWN PUBLISHERS, INC., NEW YORK

To Maurice, Carol, and Joan

Printed in the United States of America
Published simultaneously in Canada by
General Publishing Company Limited
Second Printing, June, 1973

ACKNOWLEDGMENTS

This book includes the talents and generosity of many persons. My sincere thanks go to the friendly ceramic artists who contributed photographs of their handsome works for inclusion in this volume. As earnest and sensitive craftsmen they enrich the lives of all of us with their dedication to the creation of beauty. I extend thanks and appreciation to the staffs of *Ceramics Monthly* and *Design* magazines for generous permission to include in this work articles and photographs of mine which have appeared in their magazines. My gratitude goes to the Education and Research Department of American Crafts Council for many favors and to museums and art institutes for photographs of valuable ceramic art objects from their collections. Thanks also to Gail Kristensen, Ruth Tepping, and Thomas Shafer for professional favors, and to Chester Hollins who enthusiastically carved pattern paddles to my specifications. Finally, my special appreciation goes to my husband, Maurice, for his patient cooperation.   P.R.

All projects are demonstrated by Polly Rothenberg unless otherwise indicated.

CONTRIBUTING ARTISTS

Helen Barlow
Patti Warashina Bauer
David Black
Paul Bogatay
Justin Brady
Victor Brosz
René Buthaud
Larry Calhoun
Linda Coghill
Raul Coronel
Willis (Bing) Davis
Lucien den Arend
Louis Dlugosz
Laura Dunn
Vivienne Eisner
Jack Feltman
Michael Frimkess
Verne Funk
Ruby Glick
John Glick
M. E. Goslee
Raymond Grimm
Maurice Grossman
Dick Hay
Dorothy Larson Hotchkiss

Harold Wesley Hunsicker
Gail Kristensen
Elly Kuch
Charles Lakofsky
Julie Larson
Tyrone Larson
Douglas Lowry
Patrick McCormick
Leza McVey
Lois Maher
Arno Malinowski
Joan Martin
Patriciu Mateescu
Barbara Muenger
Kimpei Nakamura
Donald Olstad
Miska Petersham
Pablo Picasso
Robert Piepenburg
Maryrose Pilcher
Donald Pilcher
Joanna Price
Wilber Price
Paul Rayar
Bob Richardson

Polly Rothenberg
Maurice Rothenberg
Donald Schaumburg
Mary Scheier
Edwin Scheier
Randall Schmidt
Norman Schulman
Thomas Sellers
Thomas Shafer
Jesse Silk
Peter Slusarski
Gerda Spurey
Kurt Spurey
Susanne Stephenson
John Stephenson
Petr Svoboda
Donald P. Taylor
Ruth Tepping
Anne Van Kleeck
Nicholas Vergette
Aileen O. Webb
Miron Webster
Peggy Wickham
Anna Malicka Zamorska
Michi Zimmerman

CONTENTS

	Acknowledgments	v
	Contributing Artists	vi
	List of Color Plates	ix
	Foreword	x
Section 1	**INTRODUCTION**	1
	The Nature of Clay	1
	Preparation	6
	Fundamentals	10
Section 2	**POTTERY MAKING: FORMING METHODS AND PROJECTS**	22
	Pinched Forms	22
	Clay-Slab Construction	28
	Working with Coils	50
	Drape Molds	65
	Press Molds	70
	Mold Casting	80
	Throwing on the Potter's Wheel	85
	Firing the Kiln	108
Section 3	**CERAMIC DESIGN AND DECORATION**	113
	Texturing and Impressing	118
	Carved Designs	124
	The Versatile Pattern Paddle	126
	Clay Appliqué	128
	Clay Cloisonné	132
	Tooled Texture	134
	Clay Inlay	138
	Decorating with Slip (Engobes)	144
	Oxide Colorants	150
	Glazing	157
	Colored and Metallic Lusters	163
	Decorating with Lump Enamel	165

Section 4   **CERAMIC SCULPTURE**
              AND ARCHITECTURE   168
              Sculpture from
                Geometric Forms   168
              Hollowed-out Sculpture   182
              Sculpture from Clay Slabs   190
              Clay Coil Sculpture   195
              Architectural Ceramics   209

Section 5   **OTHER CERAMIC FORMS**   219
              Raku   219
              Functional Forms   233
              New Ceramic Forms   250
              Jewelry from Egyptian Paste   258

              BIBLIOGRAPHY   263
              GLOSSARY   264
              SUPPLY SOURCES   269
              INDEX   273

LIST OF COLOR PLATES

Vase with Enamel.   Polly Rothenberg.   *frontispiece*
PILGRIM BOTTLE.   Thomas Shafer.   *frontispiece*
RAMONA THE RAINMAKER.   Randall Schmidt.   *frontispiece*
Raku Mural.   Paul Rayar.   *frontispiece*
Raku Forms.   Lucien den Arend.   *opposite page 84*
Crystalline Glazed Porcelain Bottle.   Jack Feltman.   *opposite page 84*
Pattern Paddled Stoneware.   Polly Rothenberg.   *opposite page 84*
Hand-built Bottle.   Thomas Shafer.   *opposite page 84*
Stoneware Sculpture.   Elly Kuch.   *opposite page 85*
Sculptures.   Michi Zimmerman.   *opposite page 85*
Sculpture.   Patriciu Mateescu.   *opposite page 85*
Luster Glazed Porcelain Domes.   Susanne Stephenson.   *opposite page 116*
Vase.   Edwin Scheier.   *opposite page 116*
Gilded Ice Bucket.   Tyrone Larson.   *opposite page 116*
JUMP'IN AT THE MOON LODGE.   Michael Frimkess.   *opposite page 116*
Salt Glazed Stoneware.   Donald Pilcher.   *opposite page 117*
STRATA POT.   Julie Larson.   *opposite page 117*
Interior Wall.   Nicholas Vergette.   *opposite page 117*

FOREWORD

Ceramic art today transcends its earlier image as a potter's craft. Smoothly sophisticated, even romantic works flow from the hands of a generation of craftsmen who are comfortably at home with the geometric planes and volumes of modern architecture, the sculptured contour of a finely crafted sportscar, and the bright clean hues of color television. They value carefully wrought forms and their works show it. Although in general they are turning away from slashing at the clay in abstract expressionism, they support the preference of other artists to develop their own styles, whatever they may be. They investigate and delineate inspiration from the distant past: Greek, Chinese, Hispano-Moresque, Mayan; they borrow from each whatever fulfills a vision of uncluttered form enriched with sparkling surface design.

New attitudes have resulted in a new freedom to use the abundance of materials available to craftsmen today. "What to do with it" becomes more urgent in a fast moving world than how it is compounded. Commercial clays, slips, frits, glazes, and lusters in every conceivable color and effect, formerly assigned to the hobbyist, are frankly embraced by today's alert ceramic artist. He knows that a chemical laboratory scientifically analyzes and develops an excellent product. On the other hand, those persons who enjoy a rich experience in glaze calculation and formulation can buy the best-quality screened and washed raw materials to ensure uniform results.

This book is about the ceramic art of our time and how it is formed. It does not include art history, nor does it cover the scientific compounding of clays and glazes. The illustrated step-by-step projects in the book are designed to provide a comprehensive series of clay experiences that are simple and basic. By becoming totally involved with the projects, the budding ceramist gains confidence and enthusiasm in expressing his own ideas through this delightful and benevolent medium. Throughout the pages there are photographs of handsome works, both simple and intricate, by talented professional ceramic artists, illustrating the incredible variety of their styles today. These works will be an inspiration to experienced craftsmen as well as to those persons who are just beginning to work with clay.

THE COMPLETE BOOK OF
CERAMIC ART

Ceramic vase. René Buthaud, Paris, France. 13½" high. Courtesy of the Metropolitan Museum of Art, Edward C. Moore Fund, 1969.

SECTION 1

INTRODUCTION

THE NATURE OF CLAY

Clay—formless by itself, yet ready to take almost any form demanded of it; abundant and cheap, yet objects of great value may be made from it. After centuries of serving man, it is still capable of providing fresh inspiration. Clay is direct; with no brush to get in the way, clay must be worked with the hands—pushed, pulled, and squeezed. It is spontaneous and responsive, yet demanding of great skill and technical mastery.

Paul Rayar

Every material has certain inherent qualities deriving from its uniqueness. Clay has plasticity, or the property of retaining a shape attained by pressure deformation; but when it is fired, it becomes hard and rocklike. Children working with clay feel instinctively the potential of clay's wonderful quality of plasticity. Their work is loving and simple. If you would know and understand clay, walk along a wet riverbank where there is a supply of cool clay mud. Sit down beside it and model a form with it. As your fingers manipulate the clay, you will be subtly manipulated by it. While you are sitting by the river, look along the water's edge where it has risen and then receded. The clay mud is not all one color. There are little granular speckles of darker and lighter sands in it. Smoothly rounded stones in countless sizes are embedded in the mud. There may be mellow remnants of driftwood, many little sticks, tangled bits of weeds and, if you are lucky, some pieces of shells and fishbones. What a variety of designs! Pick up some of these embedded fragments and notice how they leave amusing or eccentric impressions in the mud. They are nature's press molds. Press some of these natural objects into your small clay form and study it before you throw it back to the river. Eventually you will begin to understand and love clay and to work with it sincerely as an artist. An understanding love of clay is disengaged from the forces of conformity, necessity, and technique. Although you may be obliged to turn out rows of identical shapes for profit, or to build a special piece for a show, eventually you must make some forms just for yourself, if you are to retain the freshness of spirit that builds with loving confidence and freedom.

THE ORIGIN AND CHARACTERISTICS OF CLAY

Natural clay is an abundant fine earthy powder produced by the weathering and disintegration of granitic and other feldspar-bearing rocks. The most important and abundant minerals in feldspar are silica and alumina in combination with smaller amounts of sodium, calcium, and potash. In weathering, the soluble soda, potash, and lime content of the rocks is carried away by moving water, leaving the silica and alumina chemically combined with moisture and some impurities. So we say that pure clay is a *hydrous aluminum silicate* whose chemical formula is $Al_2O_3 \cdot 2SiO_2 \cdot 2H_2O$.

Small amounts of clay in a relatively pure state are found in pockets together with the rock from which it was weathered. It is called *primary,* or *residual,* clay. But most natural clay is formed by the slow weathering of rocks that have been pulverized by frost or glacial grinding, washed by rain, blown by wind, and transported to distant places by the eroding action of moving water. It becomes mixed with decaying organic matter, minerals, and chemical material as it journeys to lower geographical levels and is finally deposited in layers. The resultant clay is *sedimentary,* or *secondary,* clay.

Certain mineral oxides in natural clays give them a wide variety of colors. Clays may be naturally gray, red, blue, or almost any color, according to their mineral content. Iron oxides, which are present in all clays to some degree (except in pure white clay), give them their characteristic earthy colors.

The processes of weathering and disintegration of rocks grind clay particles exceedingly fine. These minute particles, which are flat and platelike in shape, may be as tiny as one-thousandth of a millimeter in diameter. Their plate-shaped character allows them to cling closely together and slip around in the film of moisture that surrounds each microscopic wafer, while the clay is being worked. This ability of clay to hold a shape makes possible construction of countless ceramic objects. Although some clays found in nature are useful just as they are, the practical needs of forming and firing usually require some additions or alterations to make them useful.

CERAMIC CLAY

Ceramic clay *bodies* are blends of different clays and other substances that give them plasticity, porosity, and predictable vitrification temperatures. Ceramic clay must be plastic so it is easily shaped without crumbling or collapsing. It must be porous and open enough to dry and fire without cracking, warping, or shrinking too much. It must also contain carefully calculated amounts of fluxing agents that control the temperatures at which one may expect it to mature, or to become hard and vitreous.

The smaller the particles of clay, the smaller are the pores between them and the closer they shrink together when they are dried and fired. If the clay is dense and closely packed, it will shrink too much. Fine clays can be mixed with sand or grog to increase porosity and lessen the shrinkage of drying and firing. (Shrinkage during firing is discussed in the section on the firing cycle.)

SOME NATURAL CLAYS

Common Clays

A wide variety of common red clays cover the earth. These clays contain much iron and other mineral "impurities" that give them low maturing temperatures. Most pottery is made of this low-firing red earthenware clay, modified to suit each purpose.

Stoneware Clays

Smooth plastic sedimentary stoneware clays withstand high temperatures. They usually appear in light buff, gray, or light brown. Stoneware clay makes pleasing pottery forms that will take a variety of slips and high-firing glazes. They are often left unglazed. In general, they are leak resistant when they are fired to high vitrification temperature.

Kaolin

This highly refractory white clay is used for making white porcelain or china. Its name comes from *kao-ling,* meaning hill, or ridge, after the name of the hill in China where it was first dug as a residual, or primary, clay centuries ago. Because kaolin is formed on the parent rock site and is not transported and ground to fine dust by moving water, particles are rather coarse and nonplastic. Certain materials must

be added to it so that it is more plastic and easily shaped. Other additions to kaolin give it the hardness, whiteness, and translucence necessary for making pure white china.

COSAS. *Raul Coronel. Stoneware sculpture, wheel thrown and assembled. Iron brown, blue, white, amber, and beige. Courtesy of the artist.*

Ceramic vase. Elly Kuch, West Germany. 10″ high.
Gray ash glaze. Courtesy of the artist. Photo by Kuch.

Ball Clays

These are sedimentary clays and are consequently very fine grained, which makes them shrink excessively. Although they usually contain dark carbonaceous material, they fire nearly white. Ball clays are highly plastic and are added to kaolin to give it workability in porcelain bodies.

Fire Clay

Dark rough-textured fire clay is not very plastic. It withstands high temperatures and is useful in the manufacture of refractory brick for kilns, furnaces, boilers, and smelters. It is sometimes mixed with stoneware clay to add desirable texture.

Bentonite

This is an extremely fine plastic clay of volcanic dust origin. When it is added to clay bodies, it improves plasticity.

SOME CERAMIC BODIES

The term "cone" used in describing clay bodies refers to the temperature at which a clay reaches maturity when it is fired. Small triangular cones made of ceramic materials are compounded to bend and melt at specified kiln temperatures. Cone use and temperature tables are given under Firing.

Earthenware bodies are low firing (from cone 06 to cone 1). These ceramic clays are suitable for hand building, throwing, or modeling. An earthenware body is red, brown, or buff according to the amounts of iron oxide in the natural red clay that makes up most of the body, with only enough modification to make it workable and of good firing properties. Earthenware will not hold liquids unless it is glazed, because of its open porous nature.

Covered jar. Thomas Shafer. 18½″ high. Light earthy red. Slab built, thrown top. Courtesy of the Butler Institute of American Art.

Modeling clay bodies must dry rapidly with little chance of cracking. Twenty to 30 percent grog mixed with ball clay is a simple modeling clay that has plasticity and minimum shrinking and cracking difficulties during drying and firing.

Throwing clay bodies must be very plastic; they must stand up well and hold their shape; and they must be cohesive during throwing. A clay that is too fine grained will not stand up in tall or large thrown forms. About 8 percent of granular material such as fine grog will improve throwing clay, but too much will make it lose plasticity. Throwing clay must be porous enough to hold up under the constant wetting it undergoes as the potter lubricates his clay and hands during the throwing. To keep from over-saturating the clay, some experienced potters frequently lubricate their hands with a thin slip made from the throwing clay, instead of using plain water.

Stoneware bodies may be of natural stoneware clay or a prepared body containing high percentages of alumina and silica. They are hard when they are fired to the maturing temperature of approximately cone 8. Because they have very little iron content, they may be gray in color but fire to light buff. For texture, grog or fire clay are added.

Sculpture clay must be easy to work and must be capable of holding its shape without sagging or cracking. Stoneware and fire clay make good sculpture bodies. Bentonite (3 percent) may be added to fire clay to improve its workability. All sculpture clay bodies contain 10 percent to 30 percent grog, in 20 mesh to fine mesh size. Low-firing red earthenware sculpture clay is popular for school classes.

Porcelain is a high-firing white clay body composed chiefly of refractory kaolin combined with feldspar, flint, some fluxing material, and enough ball clay to make it more plastic. If more than 15 percent of ball clay is added, the white clay may become off-white.

Slab constructed vase. Maurice Grossman. Stoneware with white glaze, cobalt blue lines; tops are gold luster. Mr. Grossman is Professor of Art, University of Arizona at Tucson.

Bowl. Edwin and Mary Scheier. Buff stoneware. Black metallic glaze with sgraffitoed linear design. 5" high, 10" in diameter. Collection of the author.

Because it is only in recent decades that the styles of porcelain have begun to break away from the traditional, a few additional comments about this romantic material are included here.

Translucent porcelain was first developed in the Orient around A.D. 800. It was found that kaolin, its principal ingredient, and a partly decomposed feldspathic granite called "petuntse," when fired to about 1450°C, formed a hard-paste porcelain. Soft-paste porcelain, first produced in England around the middle of the eighteenth century, was chiefly a mixture of white china clay and steatite, a form of talc. Soft-paste porcelain, with a lower fusing temperature, shows a maze of fine scratching and sometimes of crazing over a period of time, but this does not detract from its appeal to porcelain collectors. Hard-paste porcelain can scarcely be scratched, even with a file.

The flamboyant baroque decorative style in Europe in the seventeenth century, and the rococo porcelain originating in France in the eighteenth century, with its curves, scrolls, and flourishes, had a sort of sophisticated opulence. Reaction against it in 1760 coincided with the return to neoclassicism felt in all the arts at the time. Subsequently, many refinements in technique and changes in style appeared as each country evolved its own indigenous porcelain.

Porcelain was introduced into the United States in the late eighteenth century. Skilled workers in translucent soft-paste porcelain came mainly from England. But in 1828, a hard-paste porcelain was developed in Pennsylvania by William Tucker and Thomas Hulme. Ten years later, a porcelain factory founded in East Liverpool, Ohio, became the largest pottery factory in the world. Simply modeled naïve figures, naturalistic figurines, "elegant" gilt and whiteware, and humorous souvenir objects, both in fine pieces and in fakes and forgeries, appeared on whatnot shelves. But overshadowing all these objects was the porcelain table setting. The glamour surrounding it became an indicator of a home's culture.

PREPARATION

Buying Clay

From the bewildering array of clays and clay techniques, the knowing craftsman selects only those that most suit his use, his temperament, and his way of working. It may be well for the novice to buy some five-pound bags of several prepared moist clay bodies and experiment with them before he invests in a large amount of ceramic clay whose properties are unknown to him.

It is important to select a clay body that suits the use for which it is intended, such as sculpture, wheel throwing, and so on. The firing capacity of the available kiln is a most important consideration. If you plan to have your pieces custom fired, check with the kiln operator before buying clay; high-firing clays require a high-firing kiln. Experienced clay craftsmen often settle on one or two clay bodies especially right for their purpose and their kiln, or they may have clay mixed by a supplier according to their own formula. Commercially mixed moist clay is de-aired in a vacuum pug mill. It has the right consistency and is compacted for immediate use. Clay can be bought from any local studio supplier in five, twenty-five, or fifty pounds of moist ready-to-use clay body packed in heavy plastic storage bags. Although this is a convenient and timesaving way to buy ceramic clay, it is less costly to purchase dry clay in larger amounts. If cost is a greater factor in the purchase of clay than time and convenience, you may prefer to buy dry clay flour that needs only the addition of water and thorough mixing.

Mixing and Storing Clay

Ready prepared, air-floated dry clay has been ground, sieved, and sacked in a very fine dust form that can be mixed with water to the desired plasticity. Small amounts of clay can be

FOUR CONTINENTS. *Porcelains modeled by Arno Malinowski for the Royal Copenhagen Porcelain Manufactory. Figures,* left to right: *Asia-Europe, Africa, America, Australia. These important porcelains mark a departure from the forms of earlier porcelain ware. Courtesy of the Cooper-Hewitt Museum of Design, Smithsonian Institution.*

Porcelain domes. Susanne G. Stephenson. White, gold, and colored lusters. Low-fire glazes, cone 020 for lusters. Mrs. Stephenson teaches at Eastern Michigan State University. Courtesy of the artist.

blended by hand with a large stick or paddle, if no machine is available for mixing. A large shallow container is partly filled with water. Sprinkle clay powder into the water gradually (not water into clay), ensuring that each particle has a chance to get wet and that the clay does not pile up into sticky lumps that are half dry, half wet. Make additions very slowly and pause occasionally so the clay has time to absorb or "slake." Stir the mix continually and add clay flour as long as you can stir.

If you use a broad shallow container, the mixture can be blended with a hoe in the manner of mixing cement. In some creative ceramics classes, enterprising students even step in with bare feet and continue to stamp and mix the clay when it becomes too stiff to be stirred. When the clay has become quite thick, it will still be too wet for immediate use. It can be scraped into large, shallow plaster basins, and excess moisture is soon absorbed. Then the clay is pulled from the plaster and stored in airtight containers. The plaster basins will become water soaked and should be set in the sun or in a warm room to dry.

Mixing clay by hand may be satisfactory for relatively small amounts, but for large production of moist clay, this method is too slow and arduous. Some kind of mixing and blending machine is necessary. Some schools use improvised mixers such as old washers, bakery dough blenders, or other heavy-duty stirring devices, and find them satisfactory. There are, of course, excellent studio pug mills designed for schools and studio potters. They mix, blend, wedge, and remix any combination of powdered clay, moist-clay chunks or scraps, and water. They can process a minimum of 100 to 300 pounds of clay an hour, depending on their capacity. Clay is ejected in perfect condition, ready for use, in a continuous rectangular block, which is cut off as it leaves the pug mill and drops into a plastic bag conveniently waiting in its metal supporting frame. The bag is sealed shut ready

Porcelain vase. Michi Zimmerman. Black iron oxide, white glaze. Courtesy of the artist.

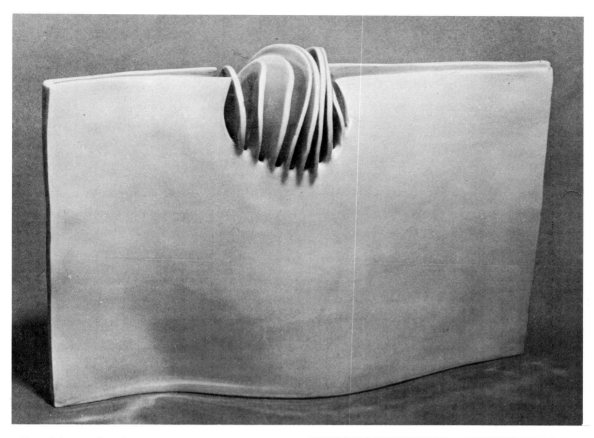

Porcelain vessel with fans. Kurt and Gerda Spurey.
Courtesy of the artists.

for storage. The serious producing ceramic craftsman finds a pug mill to be as important a piece of equipment as a kiln or throwing wheel.

Moist clay must be stored in airtight containers so it does not become dry and lose workability. Durable heavy plastic trash containers with close-fitting lids make excellent clay storage bins. Clay can be made up in small or large batches and stacked in the container. Plastic sheeting should be placed over the clay and tucked in around it before the lid is replaced. If the freshly blended clay is left to age for a week or two, its workability will be greatly improved. Some old clay should be left in the bin when newly mixed clay is added to the supply so bacterial gels that promote plasticity will multiply more rapidly, improve the clay's workability.

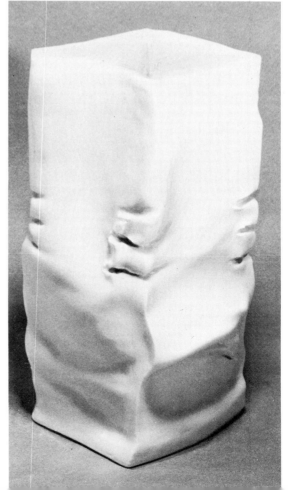

Slab-built porcelain, altered. Kurt and Gerda Spurey.
15" high. Courtesy of the artists.

Earthenware form. Patti Warashina Bauer. 2½' x 2'. Low-fire glazes (white, black, red, blue, yellow), with luster. Courtesy of the artist.

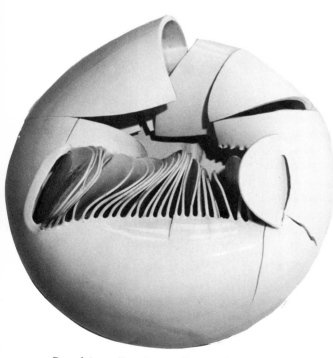

Porcelain wall sculpture. Kurt and Gerda Spurey, Austria. 12" in diameter. The piece was formed then burst to make splits. The forms are altered so the methods of construction are visible to the viewer. Courtesy of the artists.

FUNDAMENTALS

Clay particles are microscopic thin, flat, oval crystals called *flocs,* which cling closely together when moist to form a compact mass of clay. When clay is combined with adequate water, particles are said to *flocculate* and form a plastic clay that can be molded into almost any shape. If too much water is added, the clay will collapse and lose its plasticity. If too much moisture evaporates from the clay, the particles will shrink tightly together and the clay will become dense and stiff. It no longer will be workable. Clay tends to dry out from exposure to air and the heat of your hands. Lay a damp cloth or sheet of plastic over your supply of clay while you work to keep it in moist condition. Whenever you must leave your work, even for a short length of time, a sheet of plastic or an inverted plastic bag will keep it in moist condition for several days. Good moist clay, properly wedged, is a requirement for successful ceramic work, hand built or wheel thrown.

Wedging Clay

Clay is *wedged* to remove air pockets and to make clay smooth and plastic. In one wedging process, clay is kneaded by hand to make it completely plastic. Craftsmen also wedge clay by cutting and recombining the cut sections, slamming one on the other; it must be done several times until the clay is quite smooth and free of air pockets. Hard or soft parts must disappear, making the clay of even consistency. Keeping clay in workable condition is a continuous and necessary problem.

To wedge clay by kneading, both hands lift and move the clay from the outside of the mass toward the center; then they press down and push out slowly to the edge again. The mass is lifted and rotated slightly, then pressed and pushed out in a circular movement that makes flat clay particles lie parallel to one another; the clay becomes more plastic and workable.

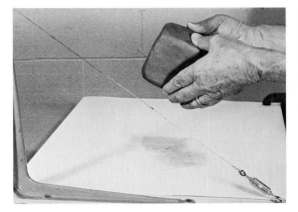

A turnbuckle keeps the wire taut so clay can be brought down over it and cut in two halves.

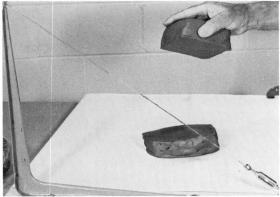

One half is thrown down, cut side up; the second half is thrown onto it with force to exclude all air bubbles. Wedged clay is formed into large balls and covered with plastic.

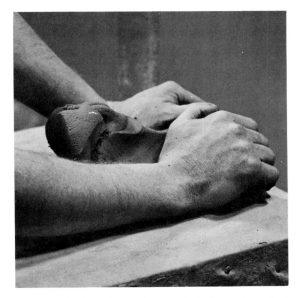

Wedging by kneading. The top of the lump is pushed forward.

To wedge clay by cutting and recombining it, a wedging board with a tautly stretched wire is advisable. But clay can be cut by placing a lump of clay on a wire and pulling the wire up through the clay. Tap a sizable lump of clay, about fist size for a first project, and form it into a cube or a rectangular block. Cut it in two fairly equal pieces with the wire, and slam one cut half on top the other with some force. Pick up and slam down two or three times, then again cut the clay over the wire. Repeat the slamming and cutting fifteen to twenty times or as often as necessary to bring the clay to a smooth homogenous mass.

If the clay seems soft and sticky, it is a little too wet. Wedge it on a canvas-covered plaster bat for several minutes and it will become workable. If a coil of clay shows cracks when it is bent double, the clay is a little too dry. Slice up the lump of clay and moisten the sections with a damp sponge. Then recombine the clay and knead or wedge it on canvas, but *not* on plaster, until it becomes smooth and plastic again. These methods of reconditioning apply only to clay that is *slightly* too wet or too dry. Clay that is completely out of condition must be reworked.

Joanna Price remixes clay in a heavy-duty Walker pug mill. The clay is ready for use after a single pass through the mill.

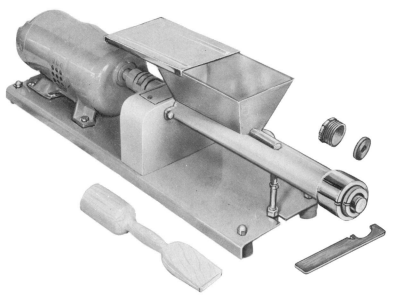

A lightweight Amaco table-model pug mill that can process approximately 100 pounds of clay an hour. Courtesy, American Art Clay Company.

MOON WEEDS. *Raymond Grimm. Welded steel and stoneware, copper oxidation glazes. Courtesy of the artist.*

Reworking Clay

Accumulations of *partly* dry clay, clay scraps, and discarded *unfired* clay objects that have become too dry to be combined with moist clay must be worked over into plastic condition. These clay scraps are collected in a galvanized or plastic tub or bucket containing some water; the clay will absorb water and soften. When the container becomes nearly full, excess water is poured off. The ideal procedure is to toss the mix into a pug mill; a single pass through the mill renders it into perfect working consistency. Unfortunately, a pug mill is not always obtainable. The clay must be reclaimed by hand on a large plaster bat and wedging board. Where large amounts of clay must be processed, hand mixing becomes untenable. If a pug mill is out of the question, some kind of improvised heavy-duty blender, such as a used dough mixer or an old washing machine, must be pressed into service.

Joining Clay

Ideally, pieces of clay that will be joined should be of equal consistency. To join moist clay sections, scratch or score the juncture areas of both pieces and paint them with slip, or *slurry*. Press them firmly together so they will not separate when they dry. A few drops of vinegar added to slurry will make it more adhesive.

To make slurry, collect a supply of small scraps of the clay you are using and dry them. Crush the dry scraps into a powder and mix it with enough water to make a thick creamy slip. Pieces of moist clay must be joined with a slurry made from the same kind of clay. Keep some slurry handy in a correctly labeled covered jar.

If clay pieces of unequal moisture content must be joined, such as a cup and handle or bowl and foot, spray the joined area and cover the completed object with a plastic bag for a day or two; capillary attraction will equalize moisture of the joined clay. The drier segment will slowly absorb moisture from the wetter portion and a successful juncture may be achieved. If a thin coating of wax emulsion, such as wax resist, is painted over the moist clay around the juncture area, it will slow down the drying and help prevent cracks at the juncture. The wax burns off in the bisque fire.

Clay slip or water containing any clay *must not be washed down the drain*. Clay particles will cling together in a dense layer in the drain pipes and will completely clog them. A container of water should be kept in the sink; tools and hands are cleaned of clay in this water. The clay will settle in the container. Clear water at the top is poured off at some suitable spot, preferably out of doors, not down the drain. Remaining soft clay is added to the clay scrap tub for reworking. Remember to keep bits of trash and other foreign material out of the clay scrap container.

Grog and Its Uses

Once clay has been fired, it cannot be softened with water or made plastic again. *Grog* is a useful material made of *fired* clay that has been crushed or ground, then screened to various mesh sizes, from fine to coarse. It is labeled according to the number of mesh openings in one square inch of the screening through which it is sieved for classification. For example, #30-mesh grog will pass through 30-mesh screening, but not through 40-mesh screen. The higher the mesh number is, the finer is the grog. It can be bought from ceramic suppliers in various colors, mesh sizes, and firing temperatures. Its uses are both technical and artistic.

When grog is combined with unfired moist clay, it encourages minute channels to form as the drying clay pulls slightly away from grog particles. Moisture can more easily work its way around and between particles to escape and evaporate. Grog also serves as a skeletal support that deters undue shrinkage of clay during drying and firing. Large ceramic sculptural forms have thick wall construction; the tendency to heavy shrinkage strains in drying are countered by addition of a 1-to-2 proportion of coarse #30-mesh grog to the clay.

Some clays are so fine and compact they are actually sticky and will not hold up well for either hand building or throwing. They must be *opened up* and made more porous by the addition of fine grog or sand. Throwing clays require a grog that is fine enough not to act as an abrasive on hands.

Besides these technical uses, grog has decided artistic qualities as a texturing agent. When the surface of an unfired grogged clay object is rubbed with a moist sponge, the covering film of clay is wiped away, revealing a rough groggy texture that is quite decorative. Grog may be pressed into the surface of a moist completed ceramic piece. Low-fusing red clay grog combined with stoneware will melt slightly when it is fired to stoneware temperatures and will produce an interesting mottle.

If you crush and pulverize fired clay to make your own grog, it is important that you are aware of the fusing temperature of your grog. It should be of a higher fusing temperature than that of the clay with which it will be blended, if you do not want it to melt when the piece is fired. Grog is usually mixed with dry clay flour. To blend grog with moist clay, slice up the clay, sprinkle some grog over each slice, then wedge it together thoroughly.

Drying and Shrinkage

The water that makes clay workable is called *water of plasticity;* it constitutes 30 to 35 percent of the weight of moist clay. As the water evaporates, clay particles shrink tightly together. The finer the particles are, the greater is the shrinkage, which tends to cause warpage and cracks. A more open clay containing coarse particles and some sand or grog will shrink much less. In general, clay may shrink from 5 to 8 percent when it dries.

When a moist clay object dries, unless some parts are thicker than others, slow *even* drying will usually present no problems other than shrinkage in average room temperatures. *Uneven* drying will cause uneven shrinkage; portions may warp or crack. Generally, clay sections should not be over one inch thick. If the clay mass is very thick or has variations in thickness, such as clay sculpture does, a moist cloth should be draped over the piece to promote even drying. Spray the cloth occasionally. The cloth may be removed from time to time for short periods. Handles, spouts, knobs, lids, arms and legs, and other appendages should especially be protected from too rapid drying. A drafty room will dry them out quickly. *Loosely* wrap small pieces of plastic or damp cloth over these projections, as well as along the top edges of bowls while they dry, to promote even drying. Support the object on even strips of wood in order that air may reach the bottom of the piece as well as its sides.

When clay is left to dry, it becomes firm and *leather hard;* although it is still very damp, it is no longer plastic. The clay can be incised, hollowed out, textured, or otherwise cut, but it cannot be manipulated. As the clay continues to dry and all the *water of plasticity* evaporates, it becomes *bone dry.*

A second kind of water in clay is chemically combined water, sometimes referred to as *chemical water.* When clay is fired, as the kiln reaches a certain temperature, considerable hydrogen and oxygen in the clay unite to form H_2O, or water, which must make its way out of the clay (this process is discussed more completely in the section on the firing of clay). The clay shrinks again when it is fired. The total shrinkage in drying and firing—as much as 15 to 20 percent—must be anticipated in planning the size of a ceramic object.

Plaster Bats

Plaster bats are used extensively in ceramic art. Shallow plaster basins absorb excess moisture from slip or wet clay. Small round plaster bats are useful for holding work while it is being built and when it is left to dry; the bat may be placed on a bench wheel head and rotated so all sides are easily seen. A large firm plaster bat makes a good wedging surface. Plaster slabs placed on the shelves in a damp box, or damp cupboard, promote even drying of unfired pieces and keep them in good condition for decorating as long as the bat is damp and the door of the cupboard remains closed.

There are four important "do's" if you would have success in making these very useful plaster bats:

1. Sift or sieve the dry plaster powder before mixing it with water.
2. Allow the plaster to *slake* or absorb in the water *before* stirring it.
3. Use correct proportion of plaster to water according to the purpose for which the bats will be used.
4. Brush plenty of *sizing* over the interior surface of forms used in making the bats.

Soap size can be bought at ceramic supply houses, but it costs less to make it yourself. *To make soap size,* Fels naphtha soap granules are quick and easy to use. Slowly pour ½ cup of the soap granules into a pan with a quart of cool water, stirring continuously as the soap powder is poured. Place the pan on a slow burner and bring the mixture to a boil, then let it simmer until the liquid is clear. Or a piece of laundry soap the size of an egg can be chipped into the water, if soap granules are not available. When the mixture is clear, add a quart of boiling water and stir. (Do *not* substitute detergent granules for soap.) Let the size cool, then pour it into pint-size widemouth jars, and cover them. This amount should make a plentiful supply. It is important to simmer the mixture until it is clear; otherwise the sizing may be lumpy and require straining. The mixture will become thick as it cools.

A section of laminated Formica-type cabinet top makes an excellent surface for the base of a frame into which plaster will be poured for bats or molds. Remnants of cabinet tops can be bought at woodworking or cabinet shops. For a rectangular or square frame, arrange four smooth boards on edge on a section of the laminated board, as illustrated in the sequence of photographs. Fasten them securely into place by pressing long coils of modeling clay along the outside of the crack between the frame boards and the base. The entire crack must be carefully covered so plaster does not leak out when it is poured into the frame. It is also important to anchor the clay by pressing it down to make a firm bond between the clay, the frame, and the base. Otherwise the frame will float on top of the plaster when it is poured and you will have a mess!

When the frame has been assembled, it is time to apply the *size*. Soap size (or sizing) facilitates removal of the completed bat without the hazard of breaking it, if it sticks. Dip a broad paintbrush into the jar of sizing. If it seems thick, daub the brush up and down vigorously to bring some moisture to the surface. Paint the inside of the frame with sizing, working it smoothly into corners. Let it dry, then apply two or more coats, allowing a short drying period in between coats. Wipe off surplus soap with a barely moist, fine sponge. Paint at least one coat over the laminated plastic base of the frame. The frame must be sized *before* the plaster is mixed.

Mixing and pouring plaster is a simple operation and it can be achieved at the first attempt if all operations are followed carefully. The first step is to calculate the amounts of water and plaster. Mix only the amount required; but if you find you have too much it can be poured into sized pie pans or into the bottom of a small plastic pail that does not need sizing or greasing. The resultant small bats can be added to your supply. There never seems to be too many of these useful small bats.

The ratio of plaster to water, depending on the purpose for which the bat will be used, should be 2½, 2¾, or 3 pounds of dry powdered potter's plaster to each quart of water. If too much plaster is used, the bat will be too dense to absorb enough water from the clay. If too little plaster is used, the bat will be fragile and easily chipped or broken. Bats for holding work can be made of 2¾ pounds of plaster to a quart of water. Plaster basins for drying out wet clay and slip can be more absorbent, 2½ pounds of plaster to the quart. For a wedging-board bat or throwing bats, a denser surface is attained with 3 or even 3½ pounds plaster to a quart of water.

In calculating quantities, 2½ pounds of dry powdered plaster dissolved in one quart of water will fill *approximately* 80 cubic inches in volume. For a rectangular or square frame, to calculate volume of the desired bat, multiply length by width by height in inches. Divide the result by 80 to find the number of quarts required. Multiply the number of quarts by 2½ pounds to find the number of pounds of dry powdered plaster required. To calculate the amount of plaster and water needed to make several small round bats, to be made by pouring plaster into metal cake or pie tins, find the amount of water needed by filling one pan to the desired height with water, measure the water, then multiply its volume by the number of pans to be filled. This will give the total amount of water required for the whole batch. Multiply the total number of quarts by 2½ pounds to find the dry plaster needed. Have some extra small pans ready in case you have some wet plaster left over. A denser mixture will fill more space.

When you have figured the amount of plaster, weigh it and *sift* it. No matter how fresh dry plaster may be, you may find many small lumps in it. If you can't locate a sieve, one can easily be made. Nail four clean boards into a frame and brace the corners with small metal braces. Staple new window screening over the frame, bringing the screen edge up around the sides of the frame. Heavy plastic adhesive tape can be applied over the cut edges of the screening to cover raw screen wires and prevent scratches to

Four smooth boards are arranged to form a rectangle; each board is fastened to the Formica base with soft clay. It is pressed firmly all along the crack between frame and base to prevent wet plaster from leaking out.

Brush soap sizing over the frame's interior and allow it to dry.

A wooden frame covered with window screening is useful for sifting powdered plaster.

your hands. Sieves like this can be made in several sizes for small or large amounts of dry plaster.

To mix plaster, measure out the water into a vessel that has a pouring spout or a corner. Sprinkle the sieved plaster into the water by handfuls (never pour water *into* dry plaster) as rapidly as you can without allowing it to cake. When all the plaster is in the water, *let it stand for two or three minutes to slake,* or absorb. This is the very important step that prevents the wet plaster from lumping. After the slaking period, stir the mixture continuously with a large wooden or plastic spoon, taking particular care to stir around the bottom edges of the container and mix thoroughly and slowly to avoid causing bubbles. The mix will seem quite thin at first, but it will thicken gradually. It may take five or more minutes for it to thicken to heavy cream consistency. When it begins to thicken, it is time to pour. Pour it into the center of the mold frame and see that it fills all corners. If it begins to pile up like soft mush, you have waited a little too long to pour it. Lift up one end of the base of the frame a fraction of an inch and rap it down smartly against the tabletop to level the plaster and bring all bubbles to the surface. Do this two or three times, first at one end of the frame, then the other, to remove all bubbles and level the plaster.

If you are pouring plaster for throwing bats, it is important that the bats are made *completely level.* If the finished bats are not level, there will be difficulty both in centering the clay on these bats and later in turning a level foot on a completed thrown form. With a carpenter's level, check the table that holds the frame to make sure the surface of the poured plaster will be level.

Allow the plaster to set for about an hour, before removing the frame. In about ten minutes, it will begin to get quite warm, an indication that plaster crystals are forming and starting the change which makes hard plaster. Wait until it cools before removing the bat from the

Scatter dry plaster slowly and evenly over the water. Allow it to slake for 3 or 4 minutes before it is mixed.

When the plaster thickens like heavy cream, it is time to pour it into the mold frame.

frame. Then remove the clay coils from around the frame and pull each board away from the freshly formed plaster bat.

To remove a bat from a small pan or round frame, turn it over; while you support one edge above the table, strike the bottom sharply with a leather mallet against a piece of board. Rap all over the bottom until the bat falls free. The fresh bats should be left to dry for a day or two before using.

Water and plaster are calculated for the round bat, then plaster is mixed and poured.

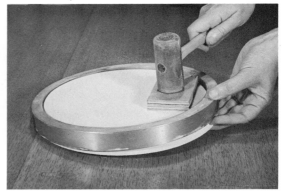

A leather mallet taps the plaster bat free of the metal mold; a piece of board protects the plaster from mallet marks.

Because this is a bat for the throwing wheel, the bat and table must be absolutely level.

Sharp corners are beveled from each bat before the plaster has hardened completely.

Pictured are throwing and modeling bats and a large plaster slab for the damp cabinet.

The Damp Box

A "damp box," or damp cupboard, is a most convenient piece of equipment. It may be elaborate or simple. Ideally, it would be a zinc-lined cupboard with a close-fitting door. But an old icebox (with latch removed for safety), a metal locker with shelves, or a lidded wooden box completely lined with aluminum foil will work very well. Any of these must contain the necessary water-soaked thick plaster slab on which to set your fresh clay piece when you must temporarily set it aside. The piece will get firm but will stay moist as long as the damp box is kept closed and the plaster stays damp. The door must be close fitting and should be kept closed except when pieces of ceramic clay are put into the cupboard or removed from it. The damp bat and closed door keep the air moist in the interior of the cupboard; pieces put into it overnight will be ready the next day for scoring, incising, and trimming. Pieces will stay in leather-hard condition indefinitely in a good damp box.

Individual damp boxes for students can be made from corrugated boxes that have one end removed. Aluminum foil is stapled all over the interior surface of the box. It can be turned upside down over a freshly formed ceramic piece to keep the clay in leather-hard condition until the next working period. If the piece is placed on a plaster bat, the bat *must be water soaked*. In a classroom where several of these *temporary* boxes are in use, boxes should be initialed for identification.

TREE FORMS. *Raymond Grimm. 2' x 2'.*
Courtesy of the artist.

Platter. Elly Kuch, West Germany. Gray clay (cone
10), white glaze over black. Courtesy of the artist.
Photo by Kuch.

ZEN GROUP. *Raul Coronel. Wheel-thrown natural stoneware, hand shaped. Iron brown, black, and white. Heights: 6', 3', 2'. Courtesy of the artist.*

SECTION 2

POTTERY MAKING:
FORMING METHODS
AND PROJECTS

PINCHED FORMS

Finger-pinched shapes can be made and enjoyed by beginner or experienced craftsman. Some of the most unusual and beautiful effects are achieved with only the hands and a lump of clay. Fine-grained plastic clay containing 10 to 15 percent of fine grog is satisfactory for making pinched forms. A ball of clay the size of an orange is a good starting size. The clay must be thoroughly wedged and damp enough to be workable, but not so soft that it loses shape as you work. The finger-pinched forms shown here are formed of red sculpture clay with 10 percent of very fine grog, purchased moist from the supplier.

Pat the lump of moist plastic clay into a smooth round ball. Cup or cradle the ball of clay in one hand and keep it cradled while you work. Push the thumb of the other hand down into the center of the clay making sure to steer it straight. Some craftsmen press the thumb down to within ⅜ inch from the bottom and work their way up, especially if the thumb is short. Others prefer to start at the top and work down so they can better see and control wall thickness. Fingers can replace the thumb as the small pot gets deeper. You can even finish the form with a small scooping device. There are surely no "rules" for making a pinched form!

The demonstration bowl is pinched from the top downward. Refrain from pinching the very top rim or it will thin too much and may likely split. A slightly thickened rim is both decorative and practical. With the thumb pressed into the center of the ball of clay, rotate the ball slowly, gently pushing the thumb outward and downward in a pressing motion. Fingers outside the ball brace and force the clay to be pinched between thumb and fingers. Turn the clay ball the width of a finger; turn and press, turn and press, rotating the ball slowly so you press uniformly, keeping the wall of even thickness. This even thickness in a pinched form is more important at first than making a very thin wall; that will come later as you gain some experience.

The heat from your hands will dry the clay somewhat and may cause stretch cracks. Dip your fingers into a bowl of water from time to time, or dab a damp sponge on the surface. Even so, small cracks may develop and these must be smoothed over and closed with moist fingers if you want to keep in control of your work. The rim is subject to tiny cracks forming as it begins to dry. Turn the form upside down on a moist cloth for a few moments until it regains moisture, then continue with your work.

Clay at the base of a small bowl can be pressed from the outside to form a shallow foot. Circle the outside of the base with your thumb and forefinger, pinching it in as you turn. When the form is completed, turn it upside down to level the rim, and allow the bowl to dry.

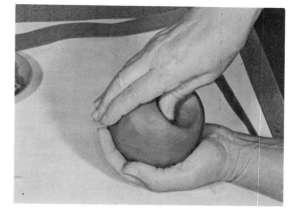

Cup or cradle the clay ball in one hand while the thumb of the other hand presses downward and outward as the ball is rotated.

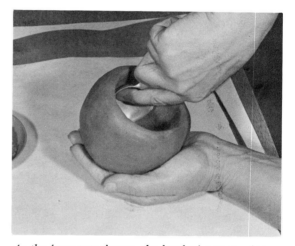

As the form gets deeper, the bowl of a measuring spoon can be used to press down and out.

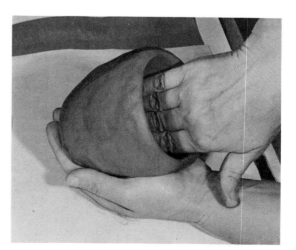

The palm of the hand can manipulate large forms.

Smooth and eliminate stretch cracks with moistened fingers.

Any lumpiness can be pinched away between thumbs and forefingers.

The rim of this bowl is curved inward, but the rim is not thinned. Too much thinning of a rim will cause it to crack.

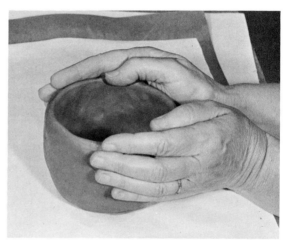

The base of the form can be flattened by smacking it down gently with cupped hands.

Turn the form upside down on a moist cloth from time to time to keep the rim moist and deter cracking.

The form is kept moist with a wet sponge patted lightly over it occasionally.

Thickness at the base is scooped away with a small spoon.

A flattened coil rim is moistened and applied. Tiny round coils are worked into corners with a modeling tool, then they are smoothed with a forefinger.

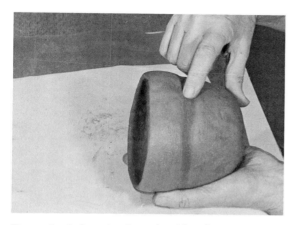

Decorative indentation is made with a finger.

There are many ways to finish a pinched form and make it decorative. It can be made square or triangular by patting the sides with a short length of board. It can be burnished or textured. Or simple glazing with one or two poured contrasting glazes might be tried after the bisque firing. (For more suggestions see the section on design.) With practice you will master the clay; very soon you will develop your own style and method of shaping and finishing a pinched form. Several of these forms can be combined for more complex projects. Two forms can be made into a covered bowl or combined and rolled around into a spherical shape. Handles, feet, rims, and other additions can make an object as complex or as simple as you like. Pinch-forming is especially suited to small sculptures.

Box and lid were cut from two pinched bowls. For a close fit, put a sheet of plastic between them and press the still flexible forms together gently.

The bisque-fired form was dip glazed. (See section on glazing.)

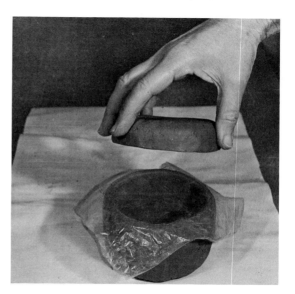

When the clay has dried slightly, but is still pliable, pat box and lid together into a squared form. This assures a close-fitting lid. Let them firm up before they are textured.

A coil applied inside the rim holds the lid in place. Tooling, applied clay, and glaze decorate the hand-shaped covered box.

WILD VEGETATION. *Gail Kristensen. Stoneware mural, 2' x 3'. The clay was pushed, pinched, and worked with heavy grog and manganese dioxide. Courtesy of the artist.*

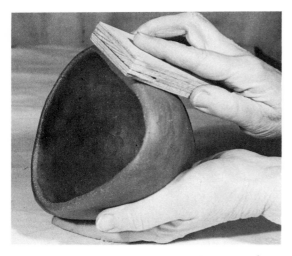

Pinched forms can be paddled into almost any shape. Support the bowl by cupping it in one hand while you paddle it with the other hand.

The paddled square form is textured with a comb and one corner of a small board. The interior is glazed in speckled blue.

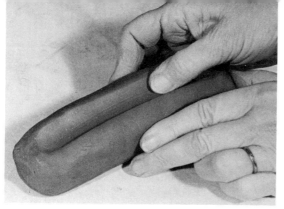

A cucumber shape is opened by sliding a thumb down the center from one end to the other.

The form is smoothed with a rubber kidney.

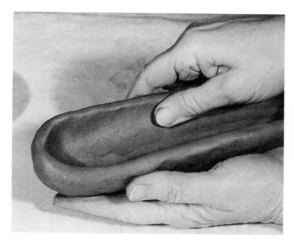

An oval bowl shape is pinched by the regular pinching method described earlier.

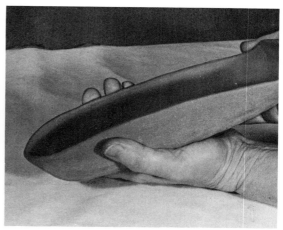

The long form may be shaped further by pressing in the sides and cupping one end.

Stoneware owls. Jack Feltman. These owls are made with a modified pinch-pot technique and sculptured. Approximately 2½" high. Courtesy of the artist.

CLAY-SLAB CONSTRUCTION

Slabs are sections of clay that have been pounded, rolled, or cut into flat shapes. Almost any kind of form can be built with these moist clay slabs. If a ceramist can visualize in detail the form he wants to shape, sometimes patterns are not a requirement. But many craftsmen make a sketch or plan, then cut out templates as cutting guides for the clay shapes. This is especially important in planning murals, commissioned pieces, or shapes that will be repeated. Any clay with 10 to 15 percent grog (20–40 mesh) is suitable for slab-built work.

Clay must be thoroughly wedged and compacted before slabs are formed. Moist clay that is blended in a vacuum pug mill may be already in condition to use, but clay scraps, leftovers, or handworked clay must be wedged again each time before use.

Although small slabs are often rolled out with a rolling pin, craftsmen who construct large forms use a different method for compacting, flattening, and cutting big slabs. They slam the clay down on a table or on the floor repeatedly and turn it over, banging it into huge, solid rectangular blocks; then they slice off slabs of the required thickness by pulling a taut wire through the length of the block of clay.

Before beginning slab work, lay a large sheet of canvas or oilcloth (shiny side down) on the worktable. For extensive hand-built ceramic work, you may decide to completely cover a worktable top with the canvas or reversed oilcloth and tack it securely all around the edge of the table. Individual slabs are rolled out on a smaller cloth placed on the large one, for ease in turning or transporting the slabs.

To roll out slabs of even thickness, select two guide sticks as thick and as long as the planned slabs. Arrange the sticks parallel and far enough apart to accommodate the width of the slabs.

Tack the sticks into place so they do not shift while you roll out the clay. They should generally be ⅜ to ¾ inches thick, depending upon the size of the object to be formed; use thick slabs for large forms, thinner slabs for small forms. Obtain the longest rolling pin you can find. If it is too short for the width of the slabs, a large pipe or other cylindrical object can be used. The roller must rest on both guide sticks to make slabs of even thickness.

Roll the clay slowly and do not press down too hard. Roll it diagonally from time to time to

Slab form. Petr Svoboda, Czechoslovakia. Pinched and welded. 12" high. Courtesy of the artist. Photo by Sirovy.

even out corners. Roll back and forth a few times, then turn the partly flattened clay over and crosswise so you are rolling it in a different direction. Continue to turn and reverse it as you roll the clay out. With practice you will soon learn to manage the clay and form slabs of even thickness. Prepare as many slabs as you think you will need for a piece and keep them uniformly moist by covering them with a sheet of plastic to keep the clay in good workable condition.

Joints of slab shapes must be well sealed so they do not open up when they are dried and fired. Allow the slabs to dry slightly so they do not collapse while you are working with them.

Edges can be either mitered or lapped where they join. If they will be mitered, they can be trimmed on a slant while they are drying, to remove excess clay. Edges to be joined are scored with shallow cross-hatching, dampened with fingers dipped into water or slip containing a little vinegar, and pressed or pinched together. Joints are further strengthened with thin coils of clay pressed along the inside angles. They are smoothed into the angles with a modeling tool or the fingers. Outside edges of the juncture are welded firmly together and may be rounded or left with distinctive finger-pressed texture.

Slab bottle. Petr Svoboda. Textured and scored. Courtesy of the artist. Photo by Sirovy.

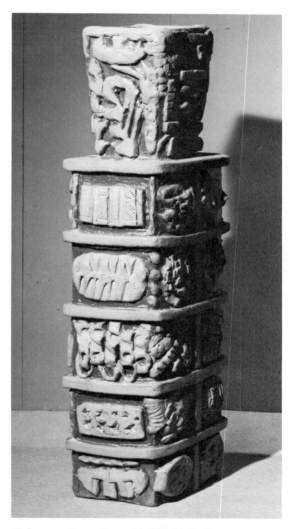

Slab vase. Peter Slusarski. 18" high. Courtesy of the Butler Institute of American Art.

Slab bottle. Petr Svoboda. Courtesy of the artist. Photo by Sirovy.

Slab Trays and Candleholders

Slab-formed trays and candleholders are functional, decorative, and easy to make. They are excellent first slab projects because only clay, a rolling pin, two guide sticks, and a knife are required. Roll out some slabs between guide sticks that are approximately ⅜ inch thick. The clay should contain 20 to 30 percent fine grog; if the clay is too dense and tight, the trays may warp in drying and in firing. Cut some slab shapes that are geometric or free form and let them dry a little while so they are easy to handle, but not stiff. If your work is interrupted and you must leave it for a longer period than is desirable, lay a sheet of plastic over the flat shapes to keep them from becoming too dry.

Decorate the trays before the edges are turned up. The trays illustrated are brushed with white engobe in very simple patterns. Additional brush decorating can be done after edges are turned up and the clay has become firm. If the trays will be used for holding food, texturing should not be deep enough for food particles to become lodged in depressions where they will be difficult to remove. Firm thick clay coils are tucked all around under the slab edges to form the sides of shallow trays. Gently press the clay down all around the inside base of each shape. Let the clay become quite leather hard before the coils are removed; otherwise the sides will flatten out, if coils are removed while the clay is still pliable.

Fascinating candleholders are made from a single small clay slab with little twists of clay added to hold the candles upright. An important thing to keep in mind when planning candleholders is to provide a flat area as a drip pad for each candle. Not all candles are dripless. For ease in cleaning, candleholders should be glazed. Unglazed holders are difficult to clean free of wax.

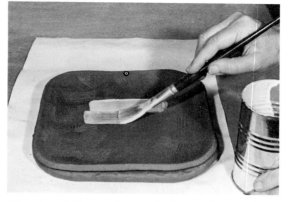

The edge of the tray is smoothed, turned up, and propped into position with a thick roll of clay. A simple design is painted with colored slip.

Clay slabs can be rolled out between guide sticks ½ inch thick.

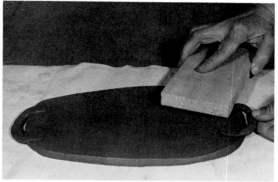

Short coils of clay are paddled into the ends of an oval slab for tray handles.

For a different method of cutting slabs, slam clay into a rectangular block that can be sliced with a cutting cord or wire.

A white slip design is brushed freely over the clay.

A slab for a square tray is scored and textured with a piece of pocket comb.

A piece of pocket comb textures the rim.

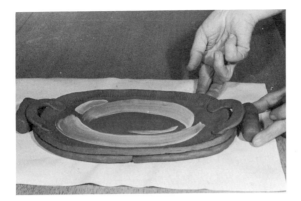

Rolls of clay are tucked under the edge for a rim; larger clay coils prop the handles higher.

A rectangular slab tray was glazed over white slip designs.

The area of the slab that will be the top center of the candleholder is textured with a piece of scored Styrofoam.

A texturing stamp makes another impression. (See Texturing and Impressing *in Section III.)*

The holder is bisque fired and glazed dark green.

The clay is scored and moistened, then a small cube of clay is pressed into place to hold a candle.

A bisque-fired candleholder has twists of clay knit to the holder with a modeling tool.

A ceramic holder for three candles.

Slab Forms from a Pattern

Plan a slab shape carefully and cut cardboard patterns with a separate pattern for each planned plane of the piece. Roll out a clay slab about ⅜ inch thick, then lay out the pattern and cut out clay replicas. When all the flat clay pieces are cut, let them dry until the clay becomes slightly firm but not leather hard. Bevel all side edges that will be joined at the seams. Score the edges and moisten them with slurry made from the same clay, then firmly press the edges together, sealing them carefully so they will not crack open later when they are dried and fired. Tiny clay coils are added along the inside of junctures and worked into the seams. Smooth all joined edges for a continuous surface; or if preferred, corners may be pinched together uniformly for a decorative effect.

On the inside of a box lid, secure strips to the lid to hold it in position when it is closed. Place the strips so there is a little play between the inside of the box and the strips, if the box interior will be glazed; glaze will make the walls thicker. When a lidded box or jar is dried or bisque fired, keep the lid in place on the receptacle to deter uneven warpage that may prevent a good fit. Areas where the box and its lid touch should be left unglazed.

A FLANGED BOX

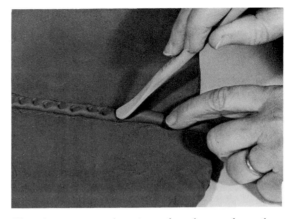

The edges are scored, moistened, and pressed together. Add tiny clay coils inside the juncture and work them smoothly into the seam.

The sides and ends of a rectangular box are cut out and textured with a comb.

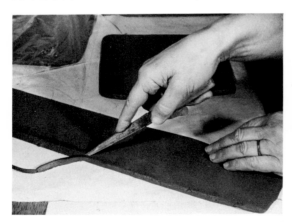

Where two slabs will be joined, edges may be beveled for a snug fit.

All the corners have been mitered and welded together. Slip is brushed along the scored edge where a base will be attached.

The box is positioned on the base that has also been scored and moistened with slip. The clay is firm but not leather hard.

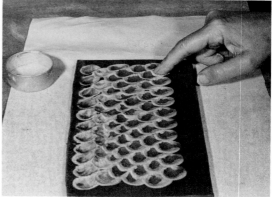

For a distinctive texture, a forefinger is dipped into white slip, then pressed repeatedly into the moist clay. A box lid is cut from this textured slab.

When the textured lid has dried enough to hold its form, it is turned over and strips are applied to hold the lid in place.

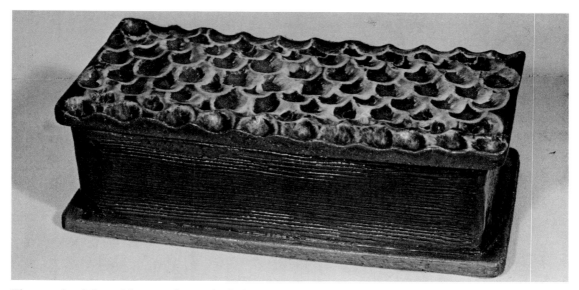

The completed flanged box was bisque fired, then glazed with transparent blue glaze.

Branch holder. Gail Kristensen. Stoneware clay with a large percentage of grog and manganese dioxide wedged in, unglazed. Slab construction, 29" high. Courtesy of the artist.

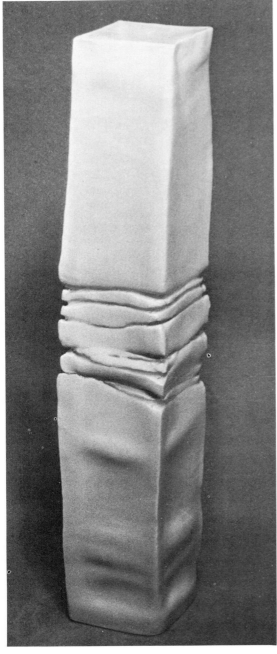

Porcelain vessel. Kurt and Gerda Spurey. Slab built, then manipulated. 12" high. Courtesy of the artists.

Stoneware vase. Gail Kristensen. Brown stoneware clay with glazed interior, 26" high. Seams are emphasized with iron oxide wash. Courtesy of the artist.

A Textured Slab Vase

Two disk-shaped pieces for the front and back of a vase and a long rectangular strip for the continuous sidepiece are cut from rolled slabs ⅜ inch thick. A shaped slab will make the shallow base. The slabs are allowed to stiffen so they will not collapse when they are worked. Some very slender coils are rolled for use in welding inside seam angles.

One of the large disks is laid flat on a plaster bat supported on a bench wheel. Its top edge is scored and painted with slip. Then the long rectangular side section is curved and set on its edge on top of the prepared perimeter of the disk, leaving a space for the top opening. Seam edges are pressed and knit together with a wooden modeling tool. One of the slender coils is worked along the inside seam angle. Coil and seam are smoothed with the fingers.

A slab is cut and shaped for the base. Its top surface fits the contour of the curved continuous side slab, while the bottom surface is flat to support the vase in an upright position. Surfaces are scored, moistened, and pressed together. The partly assembled form is covered with plastic while the front section is prepared. Because much of the surface design is formed by pushing out the design area, this area must be reinforced. A thin circular slab the size of the design area is scored on one side and painted with slip. It is pressed against the scored surface of the larger front disk immediately behind the front design area. The edge of the applied piece is smoothed and blended into the disk. Pushing and modeling on this reinforced surface can now be accomplished without the hazard of punching a hole through to the front.

The round still-plastic slab for the front of the vase is laid flat, with the top outside surface facing up. By raising it enough to slide a hand under it, the design is worked both from beneath and above. The clay must be firm enough to hold its shape, but plastic enough to avoid breaking when it is worked. The front surface is textured with coral and shells; small clay pellets are applied and textured.

The final welding coil for the inside front-seam angle is pressed into place *before* the front slab is applied; this allows for easier positioning. It is scored, slipped, and pressed into place along the edge of the side panel where the front will be applied. When seam edges are scored and moistened, the front disk is installed. With one hand thrust inside through the top opening and the other hand pressing from the outside, the final seam welding is completed. A rim band is formed and applied to the top opening. The form is scraped and sponged, then left to dry.

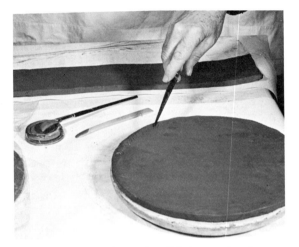

The top edge of a large clay disk is scored and moistened.

Seam edges are pressed and knit together with a modeling tool.

The inside seam angle is moistened and a thin coil is worked into the juncture.

The front panel is worked, textured, and modeled.

The base is scored, moistened, and pressed against the continuous side slab. Notice how the inside-seam juncture coil has been worked and smoothed into the angle.

The welding coil for the inside front seam is applied.

A reinforcing slab is applied to the inside of the front panel.

With one hand thrust inside through the top opening and the other hand pressing from the outside, the final seam is welded.

A rim band has been formed and smoothed into place around the top opening. The leather-hard form is left to dry.

Edges of the side panels are cut at an angle to remove some of the clay for an easier fit at the corners when they are pressed together.

A LARGE SLAB BOTTLE

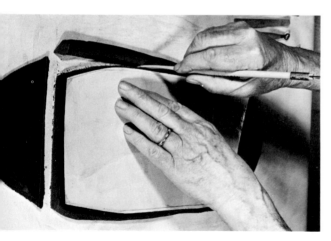

Sections for a tall slab bottle are cut from a ½-inch thick slab of grogged red clay that has been pounded, then firmly rolled out. Clay for slab work must be thoroughly compacted so it will dry and fire without sagging.

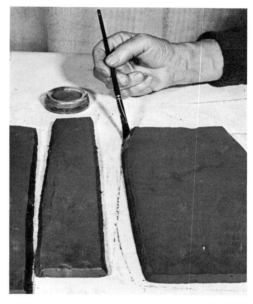

All edges are scored, then painted with thick slip made of some of the clay softened with water.

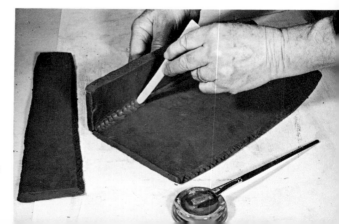

A thin coil is rolled and applied along the inside of angles; panel sides are welded firmly together with a modeling tool and the fingers.

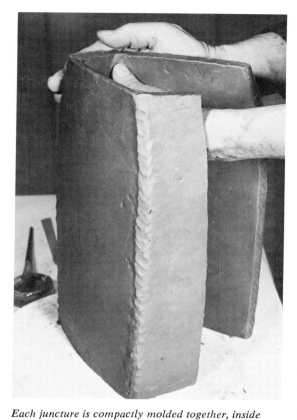

Each juncture is compactly molded together, inside and outside.

The bottle is set on a clay slab and the base is cut around the bottom edge of the bottle.

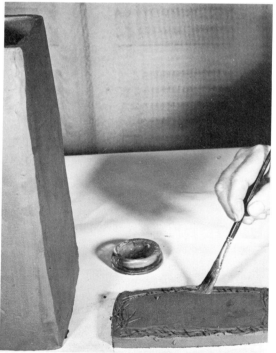

The final juncture is welded partway down, then the piece is turned upside down for easier finishing.

When the base is scored and slip-painted, the bottle is welded to it with firm pressure.

Four-part neck sections are cut out around cardboard patterns.

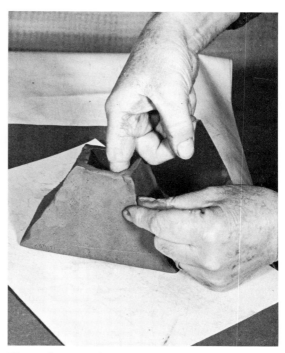

The neck is completed, molded to a pleasing curve, and joined to the lower bottle section with scored and moistened seams.

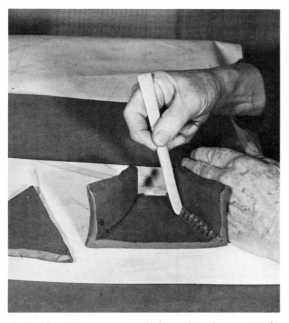

All neck sections are scored along the edges, painted with slip, and joined together with thin coils worked into inside angles. Clay is pressed firmly at the seams so it will not open during firing.

A spoon burnishes the exterior and smooths it. The simple geometric panel design is scored with a modeling tool.

The bisque-fired bottle (cone 05) is immersed twice, inside and out, for smoother application of glaze; excess water is poured off at once.

Grog in the clay gives interesting texture to the completed bottle. Project demonstrated by Maurice Rothenberg.

The designed panel is glazed with two thin coats of satin mat chartreuse glaze that allows the red clay to show through when it has been fired; the rest of the exterior is glazed dark brown opaque. The interior has three coats of clear transparent glaze poured inside, rolled around, then poured off. Final firing is cone 04.

Gail Kristensen's Slab Forms

Slab building has many forms. It is perhaps one of the most widely used and versatile of all clay processes. Gail Kristensen, painter, sculptor, enamelist, and ceramic artist, demonstrates one of her most unusual methods. It requires slabs that are not cut or tooled, except for the base, which is cut directly on a plaster bat. Only Gail's hands are used in building the large vase. As lumps of firm clay are pulled from a big wedged clay lump, she rolls and shapes each one by banging the edges against a large marble slab. Clay slabs are positioned vertically and horizontally; some are broken in half with rough edges left exposed. As Gail builds each row, she allows the clay to set slightly so the piece can maintain its own form. In order to

Slab form. Gail Kristensen. Buff stoneware slab construction, 24" high. The center core is glazed. A manganese dioxide wash emphasizes texture. Courtesy of the artist.

Stoneware vase. Gail Kristensen. Brown clay slab construction, glazed interior. The exterior seams are emphasized with iron oxide. Courtesy of the artist.

Open branch bottle. Gail Kristensen. Container for dry branches. Brown stoneware slab construction, no glaze. 26" high. Courtesy of the artist.

achieve the black basaltic character planned for this piece (which is not glazed), she begins with a standard stoneware clay; she adds extra red iron oxide and manganese dioxide granules (80–100 mesh) at the wedging stage so the overcharged iron and manganese fairly ooze from the clay when the piece is fired. It will give the ore texture she wants.

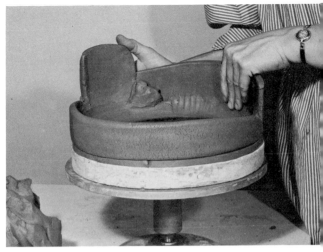

As the slabs are built up, the welding is done on the interior only.

Gail Kristensen rolls clay slabs from firm clay, then shapes them by banging their edges against the working surface.

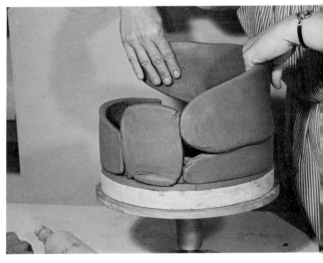

Both large and small slabs are used to give an attractive design of horizontal and vertical elements.

She welds initial slabs to the base with only soft clay coils, no slip.

Soft clay is pushed through crevices from the inside.

Some slabs are broken to shorten them. Broken slab texture is retained.

For the upper third portion, she kneads in additional manganese dioxide to lower the vitrification point of the clay. When the piece is fired, the upper third will melt slightly and begin to run over the lower portion of the form. Only experience will guide the firing temperature and time. If fired too high, the piece can collapse.*

Top view.

Notice the ore texture in the lower two-thirds of the form.

* From an article by the author, which appeared in *Ceramics Monthly.*

Thomas Shafer's Work

Thomas Shafer demonstrates the construction of his large and impressive slab jars and bottles, inspired from ancient Hispano-Moresque art. He works on two objects alternately. As the completed portions need to stiffen a little to support the next slabs, he alternates adding a strip or two to one form, then to the other. Tom's handsome ceramic forms are fired in an outdoor kiln he has built himself.

Covered jar. Thomas Shafer. Slab-built form with thrown top has white glaze with orange and brown decoration. Reduction fired to cone 10 to develop attractive speckles. Courtesy of the artist.

PILGRIM BOTTLE. *Thomas Shafer. Slab form with thrown top in white glaze with orange and brown. Cone 10 reduction. Courtesy of the artist.*

Covered jar. Thomas Shafer. Yellow glaze with brown decoration. Courtesy of the artist.

THOMAS SHAFER'S LARGE SLAB FORMS

The covered jar begins with a thrown base. He adds 2-inch-to-3-inch strips, then paddles them into shape.

Tom slips and scores the completed portion on the bottle form, adds and squeezes a strip into place, then paddles it into shape.

Returning to the jar, he adds more strips and paddles them.

To make one of his unusual decorative motifs, Tom presses a slab over an embossed plate.

He inserts the strip into the wall of the bottle.

A thrown top completes the form.

Tom continues to add slabs to the taller jar.

Both forms are completed and ready to dry.

The Shafer kiln is a 40-cubic-foot downdraft kiln built with insulating brick and an angle-iron frame. It has four natural draft burners fired on propane (5 psi). Photos by courtesy of Thomas Shafer.

WORKING WITH COILS

Interesting forms and exciting surface textures can be built with lengths of clay coils. Although clay coiling is one of the most basic methods of clay construction, beautiful and complex forms are created by talented craftsmen who use coils in unusual and imaginative ways.

Clay for coil building should be especially moist. Modeling and working with coils tends to dry out the clay because of its excessive exposure to the heat of your hands. Additional moisture can be worked into ready-prepared moist clay; slice up a lump, then sponge each slice with water and wedge it together again. Spread some oilcloth (shiny side down) or some heavy

muslin over a tabletop. Stretch it out and tack it in place. Water-spray the cloth from time to time as you roll the coils to keep them from drying out too much. Place a small sausage-shaped lump of wedged clay on the cloth and begin rolling it back and forth with the outspread palms of your hands. Roll from the center of the long lump toward the ends, separating and sliding your hands along the clay as you roll it. It takes a little knack to roll a good coil, so keep practicing until you can make enough uniform coils for the complete planned project.

A second method for coil-forming is to pound out a slab of clay a little thicker than the diameter of the planned coils; draw a wire loop tool through the clay slab from one end to the other several times until you have cut the required number of coils. This is a fast way to make a lot of uniform coil lengths. It is surprising that this method is not used more often. By pounding out the slab, you will compact the clay. After the slab is flattened, it can be rolled smooth. The top of each coil made with a loop tool will be a narrow flat strip, perfect for the bottom of the coil where it is positioned on the clay beneath it. Lay the coils between sheets of thin plastic to keep them uniformly moist while you work.

A coil form should be built on a bench wheel (banding wheel) or other revolving platform. If you do not have something like this, work on a stack of several sheets of newspaper so the clay object can be turned and worked from all sides with ease. To make a coiled bowl or vase, start with a circular flat clay slab about ½ inch thick, which will form the base. Score and moisten the edge of the clay disk with water (not slip) and position the first coil; work clay down from the coil into the base with a modeling tool; then smooth it with your finger. Each complete coil circle is separate from the succeeding one, rather than becoming a continuous spiral. Ends are cut diagonally and welded together. The top of each coil may be lightly scored and moistened as coils are positioned. To curve a form outward, each coil is slightly offset toward the outer edge of the coil beneath. To make it curve inward, the coil is set to the inside of the coil underneath it.

It is important to work the clay of each coil firmly and smoothly into the coil beneath so they do not separate when the piece is dried and fired. If you want a smooth exterior, work both sides of the coil down to the coil below. If you want the coils to show on the outside, work down only the inside of the coils. Even then you may find that there is some separation between coils on the outside of the form when the piece is fired. This separation is not necessarily unattractive, as long as it does not become a crack all the way through to the inside of the bowl. After every three or four coil layers, allow the

clay to "set up" for a while before you continue so the construction does not collapse of its own weight due to the moisture of the clay. Lay a piece of thin plastic on the top coil so it will remain damp enough for easy welding when you resume work. Different surface treatments can be achieved by working texture into the coils as you build or after the form is completed. Some of these are illustrated. Combinations of coil and slab or coil and wheel-thrown segments make unusual and exciting forms as well.

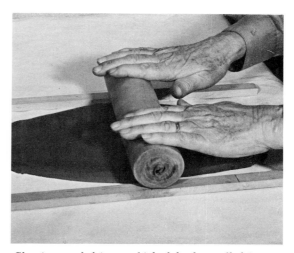

Clay is pounded into a thick slab, then rolled into uniform thickness.

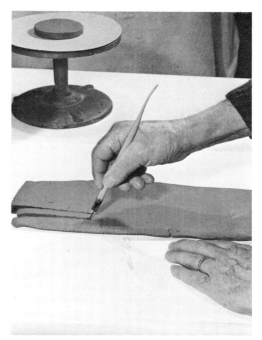

Pull a loop tool firmly through the thick clay slab.

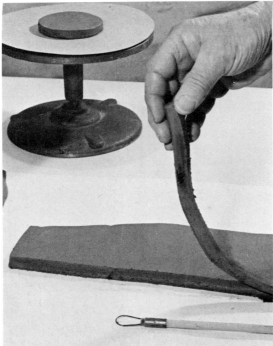

A perfectly even coil with one flat side is lifted away from the slab.

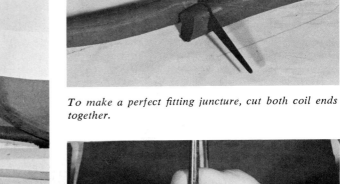

To make a perfect fitting juncture, cut both coil ends together.

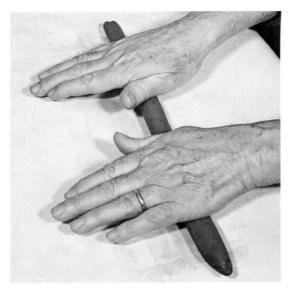

If you prefer a more rounded coil, roll the coil lightly.

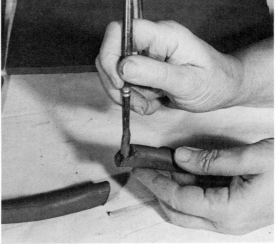

Each end is scored and painted with slip made from the same kind of clay.

The ends are dubbed together, welded, and smoothed.

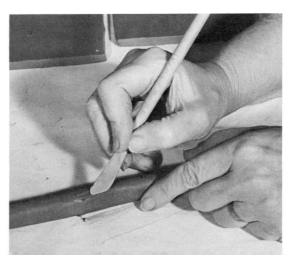

Coil form. Julie Larson. Courtesy of the artist.

AN ASYMMETRICAL COIL FORM

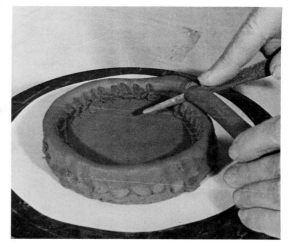

To make a smooth coil juncture, lay one end on top of the other and cut through both at once.

The coils for this form are flattened. They are welded firmly on the bowl's interior, but not on the exterior.

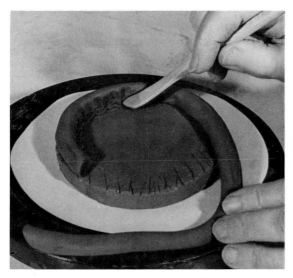

The first coil is attached to a clay disk.

Coils are worked together first with a modeling tool, then with the fingers.

The interior surface is smoothed with a rubber kidney.

The bisqued bowl will be glazed in a mat turquoise.

Shorter coils are added and shaped as the form becomes asymmetrical.

Branch bottle. Gail Kristensen. Buff stoneware coil built, 20" high. Semimat olive green glaze. Courtesy of the artist.

A sinuous pattern is achieved by careful placing of varying coil lengths.

SYMMETRICAL COIL FORMS

Score the top edge of a circular slab base and moisten it with slip; secure one end of the coil by pressing it down with a finger; cut off the coil, score and moisten the ends, and weld them firmly together. Do not use one continuous spiraling coil on this project.

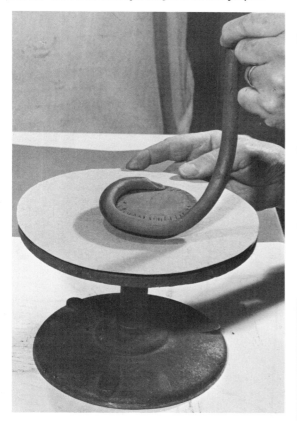

Press and weld each coil to the coil below by pulling clay down with fingers inside and outside at the same time.

For an outward curving shape, set each coil slightly to the outside of the coil beneath it; keep pressing and smoothing the clay to form a continuous wall.

The top of each coil is scored and moistened before the next coil is added.

The growing form is kept smooth and uniform with rubber kidney and wooden rib; coils set slightly toward the inside edge of each row for an inward curve. Spray clay from time to time to keep it very flexible.

After every three or four rows, let the clay dry or "set up" for a half hour or more before continuing to add coils. A cardboard template is held against the bowl's side to check and guide its progress.

The completed form is burnished all over with the backside of a tablespoon. A flat coil is added at the top for a wide rim. Keep smoothing and shaping as the form is developed.

A wet sponge smooths the surface for final modeling and brings fine grog to the surface for texture.

The surface is scored and moistened where small decorative coils are pressed into place. Because the form is rugged, the coils are not smoothed into the surface but are left with the tooling exposed.

The form is bisque fired ready for glazing.

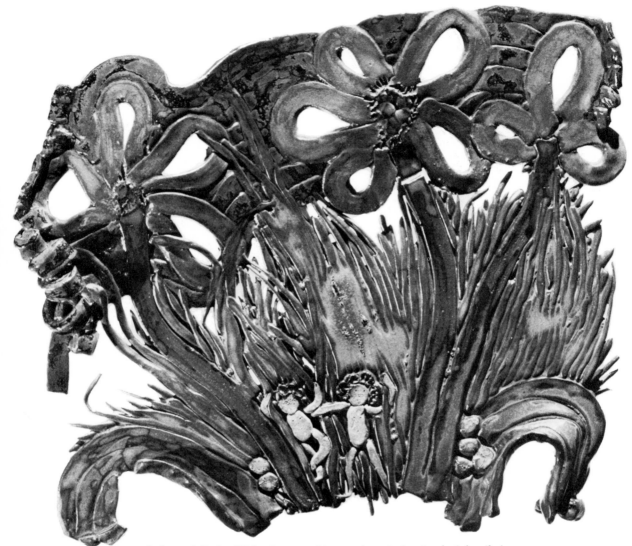

Coil panel. Ruby Glick. A composition made entirely of colorful coils in many sizes. Mrs. Glick's "little people" cavort among the clay grass and flowers on her whimsical panels. The panel is reduction-fired stoneware 15" x 13". Courtesy of the artist.

Ceramic lawn vase. Barbara Muenger. Made of tan and light blue coils and slabs, 31″ high. Courtesy of the Butler Institute of American Art.

Coiled form. Gail Kristensen. Stoneware and fire-clay construction with iron oxide wash. Courtesy of the artist.

Open Construction with Coils

Intricate openwork structures are fashioned with coils that are not welded together inside and outside the form, but are carefully scored and joined where they are positioned one against the other. Coils for large projects are usually assembled over a core of some kind. The demonstration lantern project is formed over a large 42-ounce oatmeal box. The box is covered with thin plastic, taped in place to keep

clay moisture from soaking into the cardboard and making it difficult to remove the finished clay structure. A layer of newspaper is taped around the plastic-covered box, but not covering the ends. When the construction is completed, the newspaper with coil structure in position over it can both be easily slipped up and away from the box core.

Make as many round coils as you think you will need for the entire project and carefully cover them, preferably with plastic, to keep them in workable condition. If you make coils while you work, they will shrink unevenly and result in an irregular, sagging project. The first "row" of the coil construction should be a firm slab coil that gives some stability to the project. The ends of this slab coil are scored, moistened, and joined in the usual manner. The top of each coil must be scored and moistened before the coil above it is applied. Press each coil gently but firmly against the preceding coil so there is a good juncture. Under no circumstances should the *unfired* structure be picked up by the coiled portion; for the weight of the part below your hands will pull the upper portion loose, even if it is bone dry. The hands can be placed around the bottom *slab* coil portion to lift the completed structure and place it on a base. This is very important. It is quite disheartening to try to lift the completed dry structure with hands carefully "cupped" around the coil section, only to have the entire lower section drop off from sheer weight. When an openwork coil structure has been fired, if it is properly constructed, it can be handled like any other fired ceramic form.

When the slab coil has been firmly welded together at the ends, a round coil is placed on top of it and pressed into place. Continuous circular open-coiled shapes are anchored to the box core with long straight pins. Although the clay is soft, these pins will hold the clay in place long enough to allow winding other coils in and out around them for a well-knit pattern. After every two or three rows of coiling, allow the structure to set for an hour or more, so it does not collapse under the weight of additional coils. Circular open-coil shapes must be stuffed with tissue to hold them open during the construction of several succeeding rows, or until they hold their shape. Lay a slender strip of plastic along the top coil during this setting-up period so it will stay moist; otherwise you will have a weak juncture when the next coil is applied. When the final coil has been placed, it is tooled with simple impressions. This top coil will be the bottom edge of the completed lantern.

Wait until the clay becomes firm enough to hold its shape before you try to remove the lantern from the core center. If you wait too long, the clay will have shrunk tight against the oats

box. For the final top of the lantern, cut a circular slab with a half-inch hole cut in the center to receive the light fixture. This top will serve as a base to the structure until it is fired. Place the slab on a plaster bat nearby so you can set the lantern directly on it when the piece is separated from the box core. Score and moisten the top of the slab where the lantern will rest. The next step requires some painstaking care so you may need some assistance. Before you begin to remove the coil structure from the box core, apply heavy tape along the top edge of the newspaper over which the coils are formed to make it tough enough that it will not tear when you pull it up. Take hold of the taped edge and lift the paper firmly straight upward. The paper *and* the coiled lantern should move upward together over the plastic covering of the box if you have not waited so long that the clay has shrunk. In that case, the box will have to be torn loose carefully and pulled from the clay structure. It is wise to work on a small openwork coil structure for your first project.

Coils made for the entire project are covered with plastic.

When the lantern has been welded to the round slab, it is given some decorative tooling and set aside to dry. The coiled openwork section is covered with a plastic bag that does not extend over the heavier slab section. It will keep the coils from drying out and cracking loose from the heavier portion. The bag is removed for short intervals, then replaced. To make a more reflective interior surface, a light slip can be brushed over it. The exterior can be brushed lightly with glaze or can be left unglazed.

Plastic is placed over the top coil to keep it moist while the clay "sets up" for a short time. A wad of tissue holds the open coil shape from slumping.

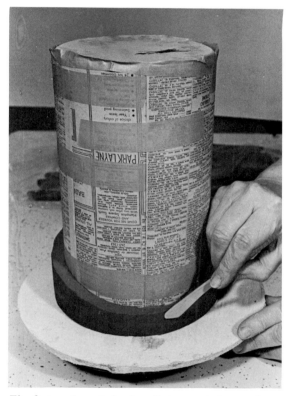

The first section of clay is coiled around the oats box and ends are carefully tooled together. This slab will be the top of the lantern.

Large straight pins anchor the open coil form to the box until additional coils can be wound around it.

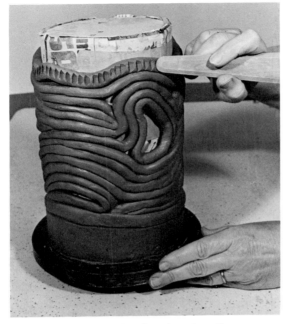

The final coil is tooled with a throwing rib.

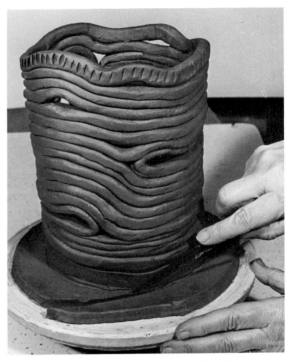

The clay form is set down on a slab which has been prepared for the top of the lantern. Excess clay is cut away with a fettling knife.

To remove the clay form from the box, the taped ends of the newspaper under the lantern are pulled slowly upward, sliding the coil construction with it. At this point some assistance may be required to hold down the box. Plastic taped to the box underneath the layer of newspaper makes it easy to remove both paper and coil construction.

All the coil work is sprayed with water because this open construction tends to dry too rapidly. The form is placed on a drying rack so air can circulate.

The open coil section is covered with plastic, but the solid slab portion is left uncovered to equalize the rate of drying. A hole is cut in the base that will become the lantern's top. A half-inch hole will allow for shrinkage and still leave enough space to accommodate the wiring for the hanging lantern. The hole may be cut before or after the slab is tooled to the lantern, while the clay is still moist.

HEAD OF CHRIST. *Louis Dlugosz. Coil-built construction, 10" wide, 20" high. Courtesy of the American Art Clay Company.*

The brown stoneware clay is painted with white slip on the interior for better light reflection. Firing is cone 8.

AESOP. *Louis Dlugosz. Terra-cotta construction, 15" high. Courtesy of the American Art Clay Company.*

DRAPE MOLDS

Moist clay draped over or shaped inside a basic form or mold and pressed against it will conform to the contours of the object. A drape mold may be a plaster casting or it may be a solid hump of clay. Cardboard boxes, blocks of Styrofoam wrapped in newspaper, field tiles, or other objects with interesting three-dimensional form can also be used as drape molds.

Clay for draping should be rather moist so it is easily manipulated without cracking. Objects that have a shiny surface, such as smooth plastic, glass, and the like, should first be covered with a moist piece of thin cloth or other separator before the clay is draped over it to facilitate easy removal of the clay when it has stiffened.

Another kind of drape mold is called a "sling mold." In this technique, a clay slab is laid flat in a sheet of open mesh fabric which is suspended by its corners inside some sort of framework. Wooden or corrugated boxes make very good suspension frames. The corners of the cloth can be tacked to a wooden frame; or they can be pressed down into slots cut in the corners of a heavy corrugated box. The clay must not be removed from a sling mold until it is quite leather hard; otherwise the clay will flatten out as it continues to dry.

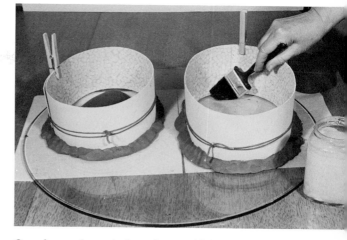

On a heavy sheet of plate glass, mold forms are fashioned of smooth linoleum strips held together by clothespins and heavy cord. They are welded to the glass base with modeling clay pressed tightly against the glass to prevent plaster from leaking out. The interior is painted with soap size.

When the size is dry, plaster is poured over the clay models to about 1½ inches above the clay.

Models for drape molds are made of solid clay that is made as smooth as possible with a rubber kidney.

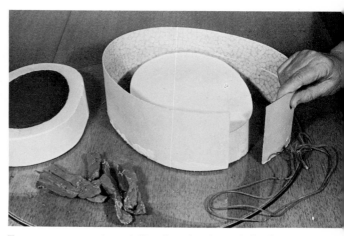

Forms are removed carefully when the plaster is hard.

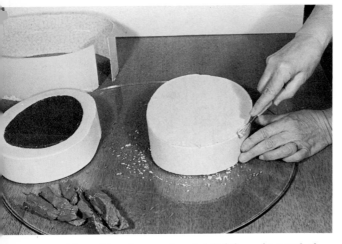

All outside edges are beveled lightly and smoothed.

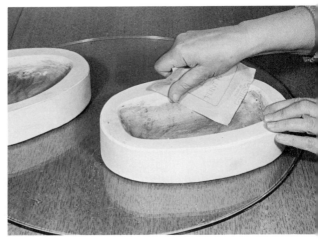

Inside edges are sanded carefully with fine wet sandpaper; the plaster surface should not be marred.

Most of the clay model is scooped out with a wire loop tool.

A FORM DRAPED OVER A PLASTER MOLD

Plenty of soap sizing must be brushed over the clean smooth interior mold surface. Let it dry before pouring plaster.

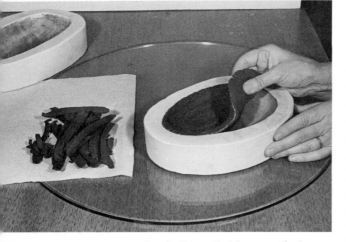

The remaining clay shell is pulled loose easily from the plaster cast.

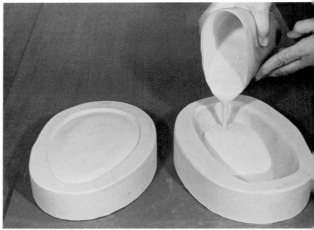

Plaster is poured into these forms to top level.

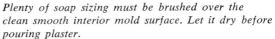

Rap the form lightly against the tabletop to release the new drape mold. Be ready to catch it so it doesn't break when it drops out! There are now molds for interior and exterior draping.

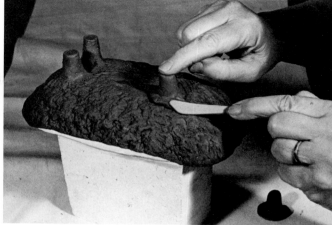

Small legs are tooled to the scored and moistened spots with a modeling tool.

A rolled slab is textured heavily with a rough stone.

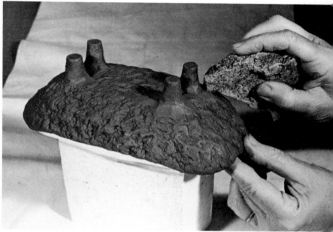

Areas around the legs are retextured with the stone.

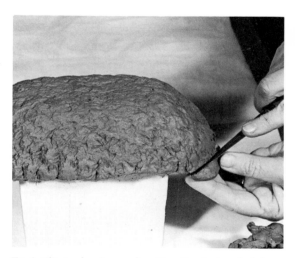

To facilitate draping and cutting the textured slab, the mold is elevated on a block of Styrofoam.

Brown stoneware is glazed inside, left unglazed outside.

Sculptor Wilbur Price alters and sculptures a thrown form.

Branch vase. Joanna and Wilber Price. Stoneware with copper green glazes. Constructed of five thrown cylinders made into one unit with slabs, draped and modeled over the cylinders. 20" high. Courtesy of the artists.

Joanna Price applies wax resist and glazes to a bottle. She throws cylinders, vases, and lamps for Wilber's sculptural additions.

Stoneware planter or lantern. Joanna and Wilber Price. Courtesy of the artists.

Branch bottle. Joanna and Wilber Price. Thrown stoneware shapes, altered and assembled. They were dried very slowly. From time to time, they were sprayed and wrapped. Tan and brown mat glazes. Courtesy of the artists.

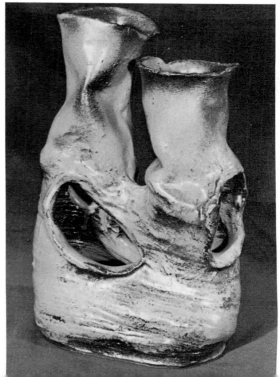

Weed vase. Joanna and Wilber Price. A thrown stoneware form was altered by adding slabs. It was distorted and textured. Courtesy of the artists.

PRESS MOLDS

Designs with shallow or high relief can be reproduced with press molds. An intricate composition that takes hours to create may be used more than once, both wholly or partly, and save the craftsman hours of repetitive labor. Press molds are indispensable for creating tile designs that will be duplicated many times in a large mural. Molds for jewelry, buttons, or segments of large mosaics are small; molds for large tiles, pottery ornamentations, and sculptural reliefs are larger and of thicker base construction. Some subtle effects can be achieved from pressings of clay made over small ornamental details of old buildings and other interesting relief fragments. These antique pressings can be applied to a variety of simple ceramic objects for rich and decorative details.

To make a press mold of plaster, all preparations should be made before the plaster is mixed. A piece of laminated plastic cabinet top or a sheet of heavy plate glass is laid flat on top a table for the base of the mold "box." The object that will be reproduced for a press mold is laid flat on this base with the decorative side facing up. Adhere it to the base with a small slab of clay which has the same general outline as the object. Press it against the glass or plastic base to anchor it firmly. To anchor news mat, tape the edge of the mat to the glass or plastic base with strips of tape. Arrange a thick wall of clay strips around the object and press it against the glass or plastic base to hold it securely, so no plaster leaks out when it is poured over the object inside the clay wall. The plaster is mixed according to directions given in the section on plaster bats. The plaster mixture can be three pounds plaster to a quart of water for a hard mold that will hold up during repeated use. To make a mold from a clay pressing, fire the clay, then proceed to make a mold from it as outlined. Plaster and clay texturing wheels and stamps are miniature press molds. They are discussed under the section Ceramic Design and Decoration.

Tiles from Press Molds

If a large number of tiles are to be made, they can be formed quickly in plaster press molds. A clay replica of each different tile is the model for making many duplicates. These same tile molds can be used for cast tiles. The background of a mold-pressed tile design can be given interesting texture if small wads of clay are worked into the mold first. For a smooth background, roll a thin slab of soft clay to cover the entire interior of the mold with a single sheet of clay; press it into all corners without tearing it. Then continue filling the tile mold with small pieces of clay pressed in tightly. When the tile is turned out of the mold, the background is smooth. Press molds filled with casting slip should have additional slip poured in from time to time to raise the level which is lowered when moisture is absorbed.

Many persons have difficulty in drying and firing tiles without warping them. A successful method of drying tiles is to lay them out on several layers of newspaper (six or eight) and cover them with an equal number of newssheets. Then lay thin boards over all. When the newspaper becomes moist, replace it with dry newssheets. The moist sheets will dry and can be reused. This is not as bothersome as it sounds. There are other methods of drying tiles when large production is concerned. Tiles can be fired without warping, if they are stilted. Racks that do not support the tile at several closely spaced points over the whole tile area usually allow sagging.

Clay relief forms are cut from patterns. The position of the forms is designated by tracing on the moist clay tile over a sketch.

The traced indentations are scored and painted with slip before the relief forms are applied. Edges are gently smoothed with moistened fingers.

Plaster edges are beveled and smoothed.

When the clay slab has become firm but not leather hard, it is positioned inside a mold frame prepared on a section of Formica board. Modeling clay is pressed tightly along cracks as described when plaster bats are made. The board frame is painted with soap size and dried.

Clay is scooped out with a wire loop tool, then the remaining shell of clay is pulled loose.

Plaster in proportions of three pounds of plaster to one quart of water will make a strong tile mold.

For textured tiles, press in many small pieces. A single slab worked into the mold will make a tile with a plain background.

Clay is scraped from the tile back with one hand while the other hand pushes against the mold.

The relief forms are textured and tooled with a modeling tool.

When the tile dries for a while it separates from the sides of the mold. Support the tile from underneath with one hand while you bang the edge with the other fist.

The same tile mold can be used as a casting mold. Stoneware slip is poured level with the top. As moisture is drawn out, more slip is poured in. The final tile will have a slightly hollow backside.

The loosened tile will drop out easily.

The stoneware tile was dried between newspapers and fired on these three pronged clay stilts; there is no warpage.

INTAGLIO-CUT TILE PRESS MOLDS

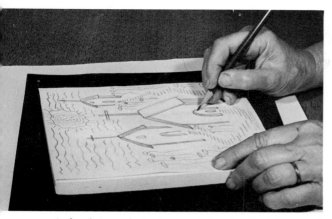

A sketch is made to the exact size of a freshly poured plaster "slab". The design is traced with light pressing over the sketch so a faint line is made in the plaster.

When the paper is removed, the impression is traced more firmly with a large pencil scoring deeper into the plaster. It may be necessary to go over the indentation two or more times to get the indented lines as deep as you want them. Brush the plaster cuttings away with a large soft watercolor brush.

To make a good impression, the clay is rolled over the plaster slab. The first pressing will have bits of plaster embedded in it, so it must be discarded.

Excess clay is cut away. While the clay is still moist and pliable, intaglio slabs can be formed into unusual and attractive three-dimensional objects.

Storage jar. Dick Hay. Symmetrical gray glazed top and lid with elliptical unglazed base. 29" high. Courtesy of the Butler Institute of American Art.

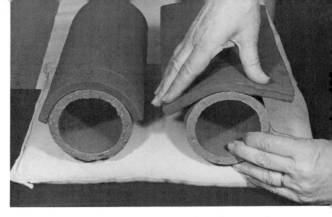

A cylinder is formed in two equal halves; because clay shrinks, a complete cylinder would be difficult to remove from the tile.

Field Tiles as Slab Molds

Field tiles are excellent molds for slab-built cylinder shapes. The tiles are available at builder supply stores for as little as fifteen cents each. They are usually sold in 3-inch and 4-inch diameters, 12 inches in length (this refers to *inside* diameter). By the time the clay is formed over a 3-inch tile, the outside circumference of the object is about 14 inches. The tiles are made of absorbent red clay.

Because clay shrinks when it dries, it is best to form the cylinder in two halves that are easily removed from the tiles when the clay has stiffened, but is not leather hard. Roll out two clay slabs of *equal thickness* and *moisture* for the half cylinders; if they are unequal, they will not combine in a satisfactory juncture when the cylinder is formed. Fit them over two separate tiles so they both dry evenly at the same time. Be sure their edges are pressed down against the tiles while they dry to a firm condition. For a tapered cylinder, cut the two slabs narrower at one end.

When the clay half cylinders are firm but not leather hard, remove them carefully from the tiles and stand them on end. Score the edges with a comb or other tool and knit the joined edges so they cannot separate. The texture of the seam may be a part of the design, or it can be evened out smooth.

Set the cylinder on a flat disk of clay and tool the edges together to form a base for the piece. Remember to score and moisten all juncture areas. One thing to keep in mind when you plan a clay cylinder shape formed over a tile is to design with dynamic texturing or other alteration, or you end up with just another field tile!

Interesting and unusual forms can be developed from cylinders shaped over tiles; short or tall lidded jars, paddled cylinders, hanging lamps or lanterns with cutout designs, just to mention a few. A variety of textures and glazes can add interest to the finished form.

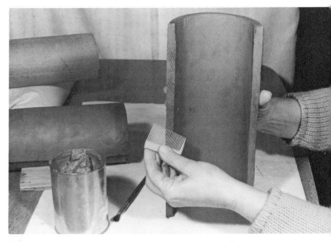

When the cylinder halves can support themselves without slumping, stand them on end; score and moisten edges.

Press and "knit" the edges firmly together with a modeling tool, then weld the form to a circular base.

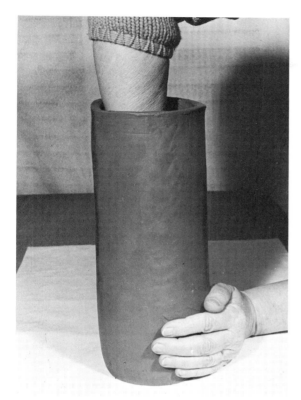

While the clay is still pliable, it can be pushed out or otherwise altered to change the form.

Thick slurry made from the same clay, with extra grog added, may be painted over the exterior for texture.

Thin textured clay slabs were applied to a firm cylinder. Glaze and lump enamel were applied for this unusual effect. (See Ceramic Design and Decoration.)

A Casting Mold as a Drape Mold

The decorative platter is a favorite form the ceramic artist never tires of creating. It is essentially the background for pictorial design. An unusual and easy method of making a platter is to roll out a clay slab and drape it over one part of a plaster casting mold. The second half is pressed firmly over the draped slab to shape it. Cut off excess clay at the edge. When the plate is firm, it can be trimmed even or left as it is and sponged smooth.

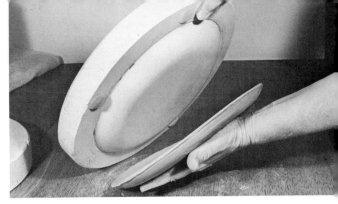

After it dries for a while, it is tapped loose.

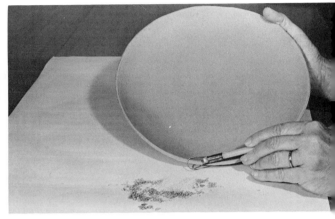

The edge is trimmed casually, then sponged to smooth it.

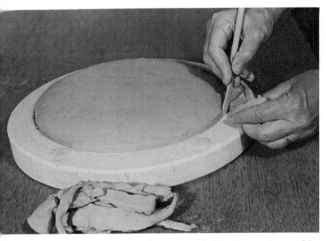

A clay slab is draped over one half of a casting mold for a plate. Excess clay is trimmed off around the edge.

The top half of the mold is pressed firmly down on the clay.

LE GROS POISSON NOIR *(The big black fish) Pablo Picasso, Vallauris, France. One of Picasso's famous fish platters. Engobe decoration on red earthenware, white base, flat black fish. For the eye, a green circle surrounding a yellow pupil with a blue iris. Painted on stock shape from the Modoura pottery. Courtesy of the Cooper-Hewitt Museum, Smithsonian Institution.*

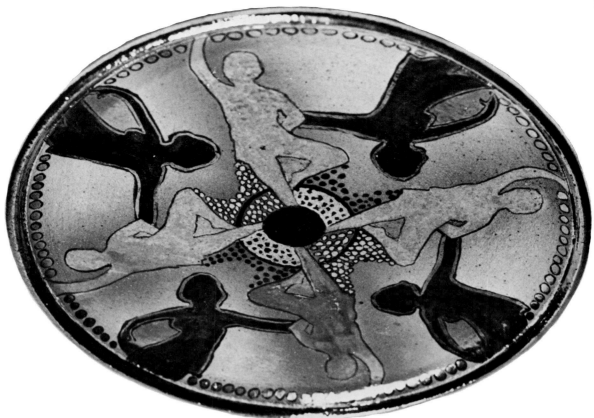

JOFREE WITH HIS HEAD DOWN. *Don Olstad. Stenciled dark blue and green underglaze. A clear glaze overall, fired. Finally, a low-fire rainbow luster over the clear glaze. Courtesy of the artist.*

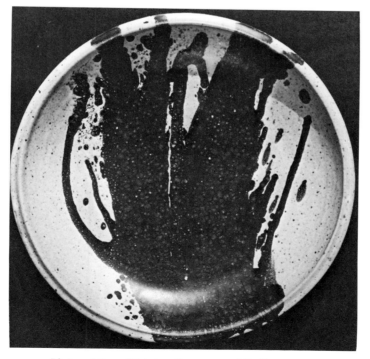

Platter. Miron Webster. Stoneware, 14" diameter. Poured glaze decoration. Courtesy of the artist.

WOMEN IN LANDSCAPE. *Don Olstad. Airbrushed underglaze on stenciled faces. Clear glaze overall, followed by more sprayed underglaze over the clear glaze to give a soft cloud effect. The plate was fired to glaze temperature. Rainbow luster over the heads was fired to cone 019. 18" diameter. Courtesy of the artist.*

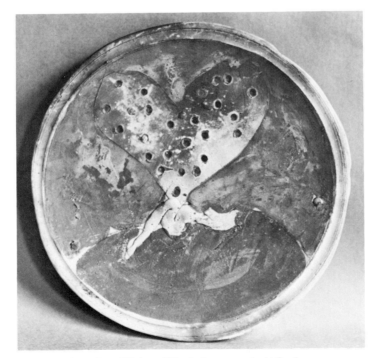

Plate. Don Pilcher. Wheel thrown and pit fired. Colored with washes of iron oxide and silver nitrate. 12" diameter. Courtesy of the artist.

Stoneware plate. Edwin Scheier. Slip and sgraffito.
18" diameter. Courtesy of the artist.

GREAT AMERICAN HIGHWAYS SERIES, IV. *Bob Richardson. Stoneware platter, 18"*
in diameter. Cone 10 firing followed by cone 019 luster firing. Gray rim,
textured area in red iron oxide, silver and gold luster highway, with silver and
copper luster sun. Courtesy of the artist.

MOLD CASTING

Casting molds are made by special moldmakers. A ceramist who has a studio shop may have molds made from his own special models, or he may select molds from the wide variety offered by suppliers. Slip cast greenware (unfired castware) serves well those persons who are more interested in decorating forms than in making them.

As described earlier, clay particles are plate-like "flocs" that cling closely together to make clay plastic. A casting slip is a water-based liquid clay body that has been *de-flocculated* with a solution, usually liquid silicate of soda, to break the attraction between clay flocs so they will hang in suspension. New slip must be aged at least a week or longer and be of a thin pouring viscosity. Before using clay slip, stir it thoroughly. Avoid beating it and forming bubbles that could become pinholes in the completed greenware. When casting slip has been poured several times, it becomes lumpy. If it is stirred, the lumps disappear and the slip thickens. Be wary of adding plain water to thin it—this may ruin its casting properties. To thin thickened casting slip, make a solution of one teaspoon silicate of soda dissolved in ¼ cup hot water. Add half the solution to a gallon of thickened slip and stir it well; if more solution is needed, add a little at a time, stirring it continually.

A container for pouring slip into a mold should have a rounded spout. The stream of slip must pour into the mold *without pause* and without dribbling or splashing. Molds should be scrupulously clean, as any stray surface particles will become embedded in the surface of the newly cast ware. Wipe the mold out with a wet sponge. Securely bind all mold parts together with two to eight heavy rubber mold bands, depending on the size and number of mold sections. Avoid chipping plaster edges. When everything is in readiness, fill the mold to the top level of the waste section with a steady stream of slip and without any pause that would cause the formation of wrinkle lines on the surface of the casting.

The mold will begin absorbing moisture from the slip instantly; clay will be deposited uniformly on the inside walls of the mold. Because the level of the slip will become lower as water is absorbed, more slip must be added to keep it well above the point where the waste section joins the main casting. Test wall thickness frequently by cutting into the edge of the waste section. When the desired wall thickness is achieved, pour out excess slip, taking care to let air into the cavity lest a vacuum pulls the cast loose prematurely, causing warpage. Invert the mold over a container to drain and prop it at a slight angle so drip lumps do not form on the inside surface of the casting. When the clay stops draining, turn the mold right side up. As soon as the clay has lost its shine, skim away excess clay from the mold's exterior with a rubber kidney. Any shiny spots that remain are soft runny clay and they must be allowed to "set" or become dull before the casting is disturbed. Cut away the clay waste section with a wooden modeling tool or plastic casting knife. Care must be taken to avoid scratching the plaster mold. Remove the mold bands and test to see if a section can be pulled open. Lift off the mold section that lets go first. If the open face of the mold is rapped along the edge, the casting can be jarred loose.

When the casting sticks to the mold in spots after several forms have been cast, the mold has become water soaked and must be left to dry for several days. Because the mold's inside surface is easily damaged, it should be wiped clean carefully and protected from scratches if you want to lengthen the life of its usefulness. Allow at least a day for the new casting to dry to "leather hard." Seam lines are carefully cleaned with an abrasive screen and cleanup tool. When all clay dust has been wiped away, the form is ready for decorating and glazing.

CASTING A PLATE

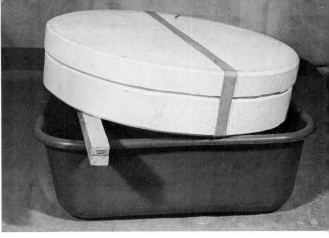

Prop up one end of the mold so drip "knobs" do not form on the plate. When draining has ceased, turn the form over and leave it until all shininess has disappeared from the clay.

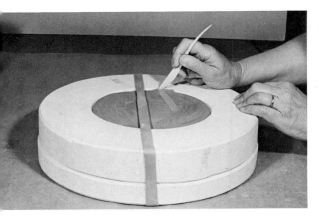

The space for a plate form is very narrow. The slip should be thin enough that it does not pile up and clog the opening. (For directions on thinning slip, see text.) Slip-pouring container is a plastic one-gallon distilled-water bottle. Pour steadily without pause.

With a rubber kidney, skim off excess clay. Carefully cut loose the waste section wall.

Test thickness by cutting into waste section at intervals.

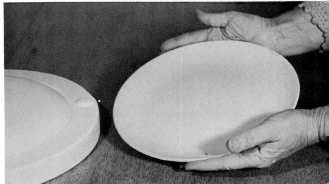

The mold is wiped clean as soon as the plate is removed from it. When the plate has firmed, it can be turned upside down gently to straighten rim.

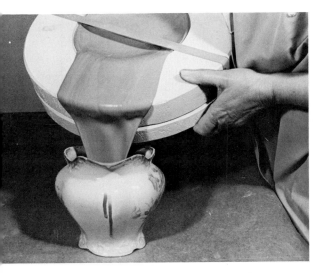

When desired wall thickness is attained, pour off excess slip.

MOLD CASTING AT CROSS CREEK CERAMICS

A covered jar mold has two parts for casting three pieces. When banded together, the mold fits tightly together, leaving only a small seam line to be cleaned off later.

A mold is positioned on the casting table with pouring holes up so liquid clay slip can be slowly and evenly poured into the mold. Any pouring variation would leave an undesirable ring around the piece, which would have to be cleaned off later.

When the two mold sections have been fitted carefully together to avoid chipping the plaster, heavy rubber bands are stretched into place.

The slip is watched to make certain it does not sink lower than the waste section. More slip may be added.

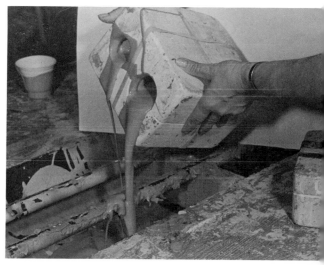

Excess slip is poured into a trough in the center of casting table; then the mold is left upside down long enough to drain, leaving a clay shell inside called "greenware." When pieces have been removed from their mold and are dry enough to hold their shape, they are put on drying racks and carts.

Forms that require more than one mold are stuck together with slip as soon as they are removed from the mold. Mary Hickey (left) and Pauline Graup (right) assemble new castware at Cross Creek Ceramics.

When the ware is about dry, these cut areas are pushed through to speed the drying process. Scraps are useful for making jewelry and hanging mobiles.

ALTERING THE POURED FORM

Laura Dunn, eminent enamelist and proprietor of Cross Creek Ceramics in Philadelphia, demonstrates her method of creating new forms from castware. With a very sharp tool, she scores a design in the leather-hard form. Then she cuts all the way through the clay. She is careful to leave any large cut areas in place until they are dry, to deter sagging or warping.

A completed candle lantern, transformed from a cast covered jar. It has delicate overglaze decoration.

A hanging lantern in bright red is combined from two separate mold castings.

An altered form made into a large black lamp is combined with colored crushed glass; it can become a table lamp or a hanging lantern.

With a regular ceramic saw, Laura Dunn sawed out 225 diamond-shaped sections in a cast greenware vase (in the leather-hard stage) to make this handsome lamp base. The form was bisque fired, white glaze was applied and fired, then pearl luster was applied overall and fired. The base interior, lined with white parchment, is lighted from below as well as above.

Raku Forms. Lucien den Arend. *(Top left)*

Crystalline Glazed Porcelain Bottle. Jack Feltman. *(Bottom left)*

Hand-built Bottle. Thomas Shafer. *(Top right)*

Pattern Paddled Stoneware. Polly Rothenberg. *(Bottom right)*

Sculptures. Michi Zimmerman.

Sculpture. Patriciu Mateescu.

Stoneware Sculpture. Elly Kuch.

THROWING ON THE POTTER'S WHEEL

Except for those rare persons who have a natural knack for wheel-throwing, months of practice are required to master the technique of throwing a good form. A short course in wheel-throwing with a well-trained instructor can be very helpful to the beginner. Different kinds of wheels should be tried before one is bought. A wheel is a major investment and a personal piece of equipment. Its choice may influence whether or not wheel work is enjoyable for you. Some craftsmen sit while they throw; others throw from a standing position. The wheel must be level and at the correct height for throwing comfort to avoid serious back strain.

Clay should be aged for at least three weeks. It must be plastic and not too short or it may crumble or crack. It should be porous enough to absorb the water applied to it, yet smooth enough to avoid abrading the skin. About 8 percent of fine grog in the clay makes a good nonabrasive throwing clay. Too much grog will cause the clay to lose plasticity, but a clay that is too fine grained will not stand up in large or tall forms. It is evident that both the type wheel and the kind of clay are important for success in throwing on the wheel. It is recommended that the beginner buy a moist ready-to-use throwing clay from a reliable supplier rather than attempt to compound his own clay. Craftsmen with small hands or those persons who like to throw small forms will probably prefer to work with a softer clay than craftsmen who have strong hands and throw large forms.

To prepare clay for throwing, wedge it thoroughly so air pockets are removed and the clay has uniform consistency. It must be neither sticky soft nor too firm. The experienced craftsman wedges his clay just before he throws it. (Wedging is described in the section Working with Coils.) Pat some wedged clay into balls the size of medium grapefruit. As you gain experi-

ence, you will progress to larger amounts. It is advisable to prepare several balls and wrap them in plastic to keep the clay moist while you practice. A bowl of water, a needlelike clay trimmer or safety pin, a small soft sponge, wood and metal ribs, a trimming stick, and a receptacle for scraps of wet clay are placed in a convenient spot near the wheel head. With the exception of the throwing ribs, these articles can be found in most homes.

If the wheel head is metal, the clay lump is pressed down with force onto the center of the dry metal head. If the throwing head is plaster, wet it with water; otherwise the clay cannot be moved smoothly into position for centering. Dry plaster will "grab" moisture from the clay so quickly it may cause the clay either to drag against the plaster or to fly off the wheel head when it is started, instead of moving and centering easily.

When the clay is in position, as nearly in the center of the wheel head as possible, pat it into a cone shape. Squeeze just enough water over it to lubricate it so the hands move smoothly on the surface of the clay, as the wheel spins. Too much water will gradually weaken the clay and cause it to sag or even to collapse. Start the wheel moving counterclockwise at a fast speed for the first step, called "centering." There are several ways to center the clay. The method demonstrated here is one way, but it need not be considered the "best" way. As soon as you have learned to center the clay easily, you will discover you have already initiated a few variations of your own. The objective is to force or coax the clay to the exact center of the wheel so the axis of the spinning lump of clay coincides with the axis of the wheel head. Any system of centering the clay that works for you is the one to use. No forms can be thrown successfully until the clay is centered on the wheel head.

As the wheel spins rapidly, force the clay down with the left hand to stick it to the wheel; with the palm of the *wet* left hand pressing down on the clay lump, the heel of the *wet* right hand pushes gently but firmly forward against the base of the spinning clay. Thumbs overlap, wrists are firm, elbows press closely against the sides, and forearms rest on the wheel frame. Whenever possible, brace the hands together for control. Avoid pressing your hands against the wheel head itself, but keep them on the clay. If it begins to cling to your hands, dip them into the bowl of water. Don't let your hands bump helplessly over the clay as it spins, but brace your arms and exert some pressure against it to make it "flow" as you want it to do. When you release pressure on the spinning clay, relax your hands slowly. Sudden movements may knock it off center. You must control the clay rather than let it control you.

With some experience, you will learn by the "feel" when the clay is centered. At first you may have to test it. Brace a stiffened forearm on the wheel frame and move the point of a pencil or sharp stick slowly toward the spinning clay. If the space between the pencil point and the clay stays even when they are nearly touching, the clay is centered.

An alternate method of centering the clay is called "mastering." Hands are joined around the clay lump with thumbs overlapping. Squeeze the rotating clay firmly at the base until it rises in a cone shape between your hands. Force it down again by pressing the left hand down on the clay cone while the right hand braces against it at the base. Repeat this action several times, keeping the forearms braced on the wheel frame. "Mastering" the clay also contributes to further wedging and blending the clay.

Opening and Raising a Cylinder

The cylinder is basic to all thrown forms; but before a cylinder can be thrown, the spinning clay must be "opened." A small well must be made in the clay so the fingers can be inserted into it preliminary to "pulling up" the cylinder. There are several ways to open the clay. Two methods are illustrated. Place the thumbs back to back on the top center of the spinning clay, as shown. With firm steady pressure, force the two thumbs down through the center of the clay, making certain you steer straight, and stop ¾ inch from the bottom. Push your thumbs across the floor of the well to establish the inside diameter of the cylinder and to form a smooth flat bottom surface. The thumbs can be moved forward or they can be separated, each moving to opposite sides, with fingers bracing on the outside of the wall. Remember, this movement establishes the inside diameter of the cylinder, so you must plan how wide you want it to be, before you begin to "open." Keep hands wet by dipping them in water.

With the wheel set at low speed, the bent knuckle of the right forefinger presses into the base of the clay from the outside while the middle finger of the left hand supports or counters from inside the cylinder; then both moistened hands move slowly upward to stretch or raise the clay side wall. Keep thumbs braced together with hands locked in a firm C-clamp position to "pay out" the clay evenly. After one or two pulls, the middle right hand finger is substituted for the knuckled forefinger. Whenever the fingers seem to drag on the clay, dip them into water. Keep your hands on that half of the cylinder's circumference which is toward you. If they slip around to the far side, the clay form may be jerked out of shape.

The side wall is pulled up in successive gentle pulls. Avoid digging deeply into the clay as your fingers move upward at a steady even pace. At the top edge, relax hands. After one or two upward pulls, the upper portion of the cylinder may tend to flare out, the result of centrifugal force exerted by the spinning wheel head. The cylinder must be constricted at the top. Collar it gently with the hands at the wider portion, exerting some pressure to bring the flaring top back into alignment with the lower part of the cylinder. (The wheel is still spinning at slow speed.) Whenever the top flares out, wet your hands and constrict it back into shape again.

This collaring action will take some of the "spring" out of the clay, but by drawing it up again the clay's subtle spring will be restored.

If unevenness appears at the cylinder's rim, cut it off with a sharp safety pin or clay trimmer. With the wheel at slow speed, gently position the left middle finger against the inside of the rim. With the right hand, press the pin's point through the clay until it touches the inside finger. This action cuts the rim loose. It can be lifted off with a quick upward motion. Or the wheel can be stopped and the rim is easily lifted away.

When the cylinder wall has reached the desired thickness and the top has been trimmed, it is time to cut away excess clay from the outside base. A wooden modeling tool or a pointed piece of bamboo are the usual base trimmers. With the wheel at slow speed, press the tool down into the base and pull it away as you trim and slightly undercut the base. It can be further refined when it is leather hard. Cut the cylinder loose from the wheel with a tautly held wire pulled from the far side of the wheel straight under the clay base toward you. If the wheel head is metal, lift the cylinder off with clay lifters, available from ceramic supply dealers. If the wheel head is plaster, remove it from the wheel and put it aside for the clay to "set up" or dry for an hour or more. Then the clay form can be lifted off the plaster with the hands or the lifters. As soon as you have learned to center the clay, open it, and pull up a cylinder, you have gained a skill that will help you to create freely any wheel-thrown form. You will discover that your fingers are an extension of your mind when you create wheel-thrown forms. Throwing on the potter's wheel is direct. The work of each craftsman is uniquely his, as examples that follow will show vividly.

CENTERING AND OPENING THE CLAY *

A well-wedged clay ball is pressed with force onto the center of a plaster wheel head that has been generously sponged with water.

Squeeze just enough water over the clay to lubricate it so hands move smoothly. Subsequent wetting is done by dipping the hands into water.

The wheel is started counterclockwise at fast speed. With hands positioned as shown, press down with the left thumb as the heel of the right hand pushes forward against the clay to center it. Gently press and release hands, press and release until the clay is spinning centered and true. Arms press against body, forearms brace on the wheel frame.

*All throwing sequences are demonstrated by the author.

To open the clay, set the wheel at fast speed; with both thumbs, press down in the center of the spinning clay to approximately ¾ inch from the bottom, taking care to steer straight. Third and fourth fingers ride the wheel head as fingertips brace together. The wheel is shown in motion.

Change hand positions as shown for a different method of opening the clay. The left center finger presses flat down with the left thumb braced against the top of the right hand; the right thumb rides on the clay, third and fourth right hand fingers ride the wheel head. The hands are braced in all ways.

Lock the right forefinger around the right thumb in a knuckled position, the left middle finger bracing from within, and the left thumb braced on the right hand. A roll of clay begins to rise as locked hands pull upward together. The wheel is at "slow."

After a couple of pulls with the knuckle, the fingers may be substituted for it. Or if you prefer, you may continue using the knuckle for a while, then change to the middle finger, whichever is most comfortable at this time.

With hands in the same position, pull the left fingers toward the body. Arms are braced. The right hand braces on the outside to counter pressure from within.

To constrict the top of the cylinder, press moist hands gently inward, as shown, with the wheel still at "slow."

The trimmed clay is lifted away.

Constricting (necking in) is alternated with pulling up the clay.

A wooden throwing rib with a right-angled corner smooths the side of the cylinder.

To remove excess clay, keep the wheel on slow speed, and press a pointed trimming tool into the clay with its point slanted away from you.

Raul Coronel, eminent California sculptor, works at the wheel on one of his impressive forms. Great skill and talent are required to create these monumental sculptures. Courtesy of the artist. Photo by Sam Calder.

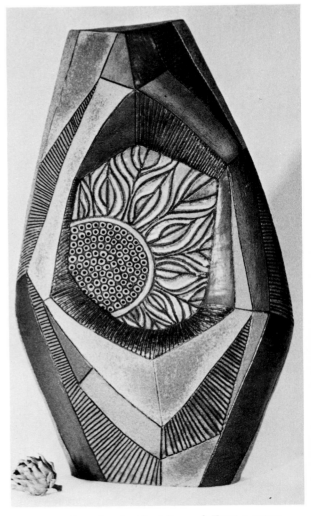

Hanging sculptural units. Raul Coronel. From a group of several sculptures made for and installed in the Landmark Hotel, Las Vegas, Nevada. They were wheel thrown, flattened, reshaped, textured, and cut. 7' high. Polychromatic color. Courtesy of the artist.

THROWING A PLATE OR LOW BOWL

A clay lump is centered and flattened.

A narrow rounded end of a wooden rib is pressed under the spinning clay disk while it pushes in to raise a low rim. For a plate form the rim is left low.

For a decorative effect, throwing rings are made with a braced forefinger, wide rings in the center, narrower rings toward the edge.

A shallow bowl has a higher rim; push in a little further. Smooth the edge with a sponge or chamois.

The plate rim is evened with a modeling tool.

Low bowl. Thomas Shafer. White glaze with blue, orange, and brown wax resist decoration. Cone 10 reduction fired. 14" diameter. Courtesy of the artist.

Bowl. Thomas Shafer. White glaze with wax resist decoration in blue, orange, and brown. Cone 10. 14" diameter. Courtesy of the artist.

Covered casserole. Donald Pilcher. Wheel thrown. The applied sculptural slab work on the lid is decorative, not structural. Salt glaze over cobalt carbonate wash. Mr. Pilcher teaches art at the University of Illinois at Urbana. Courtesy of the artist.

THROWING BOWLS

A lump of clay has been centered. With hands positioned as shown, the right-hand fingers press down and out on the left thumb to open a bowl with a continuous curved interior.

When full open form is achieved, a rim is flattened with the left forefinger pressing down on a small sponge held in the right hand. Hands are braced together, arms against the wheel frame.

The bowl is opened in successive movements, each stroke going deeper and wider. Hands are locked together. The third and fourth left-hand fingers ride the wheel head.

For a larger deep bowl, locked hands pull a cylinder outward.

Excess clay is cut away from the base with a wooden tool. The wheel is in motion. Notice how the hands are braced; the right thumb pushes up on the tool's upper end for firm control as the lower end is pressed down.

For a smooth surface, a sponge is braced against left fingers.

A cutaway shows locked hand positions and shaping of the wall form. Sponges are useful for controlling clay when throwing underneath an overhang.

Fingers pressing lightly shape the rim.

A rubber kidney is an excellent tool for shaping curves. The left hand presses out to counter the kidney.

Throwing Curved Forms

The wall thickness of a thrown form is even except at the base, where it is thicker. As the shape is thrown, the clay with its spiral growth is payed out evenly by the fingers. When the clay curves outward, it gains less height but remains of even thickness as long as the fingers are *braced in the same position.* As the shape narrows, the clay must be pulled up higher. When clay is constricted, it must always be drawn up again to thin it out and restore "spring." When clay is thrown on the wheel, clay "flocs" are forced into parallel position. This compression gives a tensile strength to clay called "spring," which makes it possible for very large forms to maintain their shape without slumping, even though walls may be thin.

To curve a shape outward, the inside (or left) hand exerts the greater pressure and rides a little higher than the outside hand; to curve a shape inward, the outer (or right) hand fingers exert the greater pressure and ride a little higher. Trim the top early and frequently. When you turn in a shoulder, do not "collar" the clay in a constricting movement or it may lose spring and collapse. To turn in the shoulder, with the wheel at low speed, position the left hand inside the wall so it is *palm up* with the middle finger tip nearly touching the point at which the shoulder will turn in. Gently move the flattened right hand fingers over the shoulder portion of the clay wall, pressing lightly to gradually flatten it against the upturned fingers of the left hand as both hands move to the left toward the center of the piece. The top opening of the form will narrow itself as the shoulder is turned in. A slight thickness at the rim of any piece is both decorative and practical. Smooth the rim and thicken it by riding a moist piece of chamois over the lip with the wheel still turning at low speed. The edge of the opening can be turned up between the two forefingers. When you are throwing any forms, avoid erratic finger ridges (throwing rings). They should be regular, rhythmic, and in scale with the size of the object.

Before the neck is collared in too far, water is soaked up from the interior with a sponge tied to a stick.

A THROWN BOTTLE

A cylinder is pushed out below and constricted above.

Hands are kept moist as the form is collared. Each time after collaring, clay must be "pulled up" to restore its spring.

The top is trimmed frequently.

Further shaping and smoothing are done with a moist firm sponge. Hands and arms are braced; touch is very light.

As the neck gets narrower, the inside of the wall is pulled up with the left forefinger. Very tiny necks are sometimes pulled up with a pencil or even a toothpick.

The final rim plane is adjusted with the left forefinger.

The neck is constricted, leaving a slight flare at top.

Clay is trimmed from the base with a bamboo trimmer. Hands are locked against bamboo trimming stick.

The bottle is left to dry awhile on the plaster, then it is removed with metal lifters.

THE LARSONS AT WORK

Julie Larson shapes a bottle rim with particular care. Julie and her husband, Tyrone, strive to make "the most beautiful and perfect forms we possibly can." Courtesy of the artist. Photo by Bob Vigiletti.

Covered pedestal compote. Julie Larson. Stoneware clay with feldspathic glaze; rust red stain streaking to black. Cone 10 reduction fired. Platinum luster on foot, knob, and center. Knobs and pedestal are thrown directly on the lid and base. 8" high, 7" diameter. Courtesy of the artist.

Tyrone decorates a tall lidded jar. Tyrone and his wife, Julie, are full-time producing craftsmen. Each form receives full attention. Courtesy of the artist. Photo by Bob Vigiletti.

Clay is cut away at the base; and the form is further refined. The rim is smoothed with an elephant ear sponge.

Gilded covered ice bucket. Tyrone Larson. Stoneware clay with feldspathic glaze; iron and rutile stained circles with small cobalt blue circles. Exterior, excluding circles, covered with 23K gold luster. Courtesy of the artist. Photo by Bob Vigiletti.

To form a pouring spout, the left thumb and forefinger press in deeply while the right forefinger pulls an ample spout.

THROWING A PITCHER

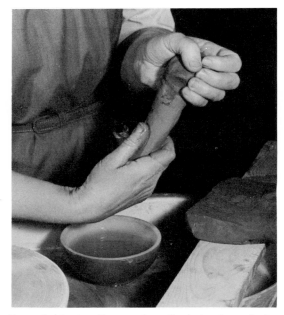

A cylinder is pulled up and pushed out at the base.

To make the handle, a moist roll of clay is stroked into a long "tail."

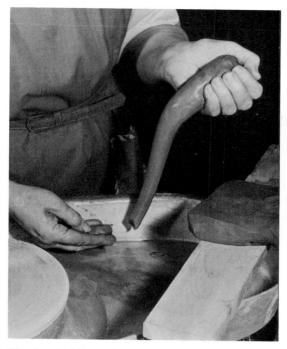

The thumbed flat end is pinched off. The top end of the handle must be cut so the handle rises gracefully before it curves downward. Let it dry a short while before you apply it. (Experienced clay craftsmen pull a handle quickly and apply it as soon as the pitcher is formed.) Stick the end of the handle to a clay lump while it sets.

THROWING A FLANGED BOWL WITH LID

To make an inside flange, pull clay down from a thick rim with a modeling tool while a thin elephant ear sponge wrapped over the right forefinger presses from the outside.

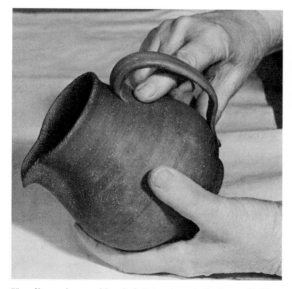

Handle ends are blended into the pitcher's wall. For a casual effect, joint marks can be left.

A sponge smooths and shapes the rim.

With no foot to the bowl, the bottom surface must be smoothed. Moist lumps of clay (keys) are pressed against the plaster wheel head to hold the centered form. The plaster should be moistened.

To check the centering, start the wheel and move a pencil toward the spinning form. Notice how hands are braced and locked. If the space between pencil and clay form stays even, the bowl is centered. If it is not centered, loosen the clay keys and tap the form lightly to center it.

The method of bracing hands for trimming the base is shown. With forearms against the wheel frame, and hands locked over one another and the tool, the left thumb pushes up on the top end of the tool to exert and control downward pressure of the cutting loop. Press the tool into the center of the spinning disk and pull toward you, slightly to the right.

The cutting rings in the clay make a good finish.

To make a lid, flatten a lump of clay.

Raise the flange by pulling some clay from the flattened disk. With the loop tool, remove excess clay for a smooth finish.

The edge is shaped with a flat wooden tool that has rounded corners.

The width of the bowl top is measured with improvised calipers made in a few minutes from cherrywood and a bolt secured with a wing nut. Very efficient adjustable wood or metal calipers can be purchased from suppliers.

The lid is measured for size with the calipers. Excess rim clay is cut away with a pointed tool.

The edge is smoothed. Hands are always braced and locked.

A wet chamois smooths the flange.

A THROWN FORM WITH A SHOULDER

A larger clay ball is thrown down forcefully.

For the large form, a different centering method is applied. The right hand pushes in forcefully with third and fourth fingers bracing by riding against the wheel head. Left hand controls the clay.

The clay is opened with the right hand pulling while the left hand braces.

The cylinder takes shape as the left hand pushes out, then up.

A shoulder is formed by the right hand fingers riding over the inside left middle finger.

The clay is forced into shape with a wooden rib. The left thumb is braced on the rib.

With a light touch, fingertips turn up a rim.

TRIMMING A FOOT RIM

A good turning tool has two thin sharp double-edged cutting blades of firm steel, one a round loop end, the other a squared end. The bowl's foot rim is defined first. Set it off by cutting inside and outside with the round loop end of the tool, holding the tool as shown. Wheel speed is slow.

The round end of the blade is brought down against the clay near right of center; pull it firmly toward you at slow even speed, moving slightly to the right. Cut very shallowly, skimming a light spiral away from the center. After recutting several times, test clay thickness with a pin so you check the progress of cutting and do not go too deep.

Hanging planter. Jack Feltman. The form was thrown with extra clay left at the base. Then it was turned upside down on the wheel and the belled hole was thrown. From experience, Mr. Feltman knows just how much extra clay he will need. Courtesy of the artist.

When the bottom area is clean, the excess clay outside the rim is tooled away, starting at the rim. By bending down you can "sight" the form's profile to make a logical continuous curve instead of a truncated one.

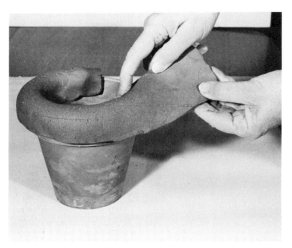

Almost any deep widemouth form makes a trimming chuck if the top edge is protected with a thick clay slab. Clay flowerpots are cheap and come in all sizes.

Leave the cutting rings; they are functional and decorative. They can be blended into the throwing rings.

The chuck is positioned, centered, and fastened to the wheel head with clay keys. The same method is used for trimming a bottle foot rim as described earlier for a bowl.

The Thrown Form as a Whole

If a form is to appear cohesive from top to bottom, the mass of the body must be as one with the base, handles, and neck. As the object begins to take shape, the skillful craftsman lets it grow or rise naturally from its base, which becomes an integral part of the whole form. The neck of a bottle or vase is the culmination of this upward flowing movement. It may end just by stopping, it may taper with grace, or it may flare into a lip. Sometimes it is cut at an angle. The shape of the form may suggest other treatments.

Handles are meant to be functional as well as artistic. Some thought should be given as to how they will function. Is there enough space between handle and pitcher to admit fingers easily? On a large pitcher, is the handle placed low enough to provide adequate leverage for pouring? The angle of slant at which the top of a pulled handle is cut and applied will deter-

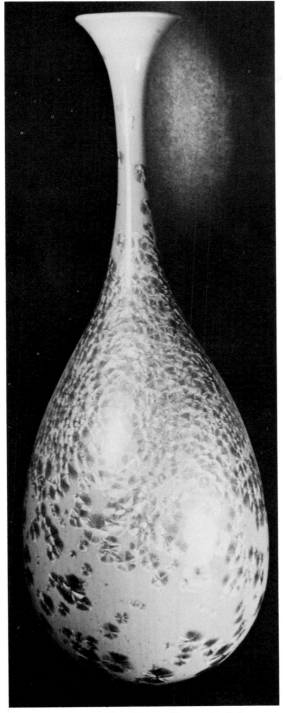

Porcelain bottle. Jack Feltman. The neck of the bottle is the culmination of an upward flowing movement, both in form and surface treatment. Crystalline glaze with green ground, blue crystals. Courtesy of the artist.

mine whether it will have "spring." Apply the top end first, after scoring and moistening juncture areas. Gently press the lower end of the handle against the sidewall of the pitcher or mug and blend the clay into the form with your fingers. (In hand-built forms where junctures show finger-pressed marks as decorative texture, handles are usually applied in a more casual direct manner.)

Spray all junctures *lightly* with water containing some vinegar, about ½ teaspoon to a pint of water. Vinegar makes clay "flocs" swell, which locks them more tightly together for a better adhesion. Cover the clay form with a plastic bag for a day or longer. If any separation has appeared between the handle and pitcher, work a little soft clay into the crack with a toothpick, then smooth the juncture with a very small moist brush. The plastic cover can be replaced from time to time to promote very slow drying. As a craftsman becomes more experienced, he will apply a handle while the main form is still very moist and thus deter the formation of cracks. Handle-forming will become a routine process.

Although lids are simple to form, the design of the knob reveals the craftsman's skill and artistic sophistication. The knob may echo some form or feature of the container it surmounts, or it may be a tiny sculpture as formal or as informal as the piece itself. Thrown knobs appear on hand-built or thrown forms, and a suitable hand-formed knob may be applied to any piece.

Some famous clay craftsmen have encountered a long struggle when they first began to learn the throwing process, so do not be discouraged if all you can manage at first is to raise a clay cylinder of even wall thickness. You will have conquered the most difficult stage of wheel work. One by one the various forms such as pitchers, bowls, and bottles will be easier to throw. Then you can concentrate on such subtleties of form as necks, spouts, variations in contour, and the like.

Teapot. Maurice Grossman. The teapot as an art form. Wheel-thrown stoneware with feldspathic glazes. Decorated with umber. Courtesy of the artist.

Maurice Grossman works at the wheel. Mr. Grossman is Professor of Art at the University of Arizona, Tucson. Courtesy of the artist.

GREEK BOTTLE. *Maurice Grossman. Stoneware with blue feldspathic glazes. Courtesy of the artist.*

Covered compote. Edwin Scheier. Brown yellow glaze. A carved handle with restrained form and appliqué decoration. Courtesy of the artist.

Covered jar. Miron Webster. Wax resist decoration. A stoneware form, cohesive in design from base to knob. Mr. Webster is Assistant Professor of Ceramics, Northern Arizona University at Flagstaff. Courtesy of the artist.

FIRING THE KILN

Preparations for successful ceramic firing procedures begin during clay construction. Clay must be wedged thoroughly to remove undesirable air pockets and possible lumpiness, joints must be well sealed, and ware must be dried completely, if trouble is to be avoided later in the kiln. It is good practice to dry completed raw ware for several days, or even for weeks in the case of large pieces, until there is no doubt the clay is dry. If all water of plasticity is not evaporated, when the clay is subjected to the heat of the kiln, steam will form and cause the piece to blow or crack apart as it is forced to make its way out between dense clay particles.

During the drying period, take care to protect rims, handles, spouts, knobs, and other projections from drying too rapidly. They should be covered with a damp cloth which is water sprayed from time to time. If these slender parts dry out more rapidly than the body of the object, cracking and warping are inevitable, if not during the drying period, then almost certainly when objects are fired. If work is interrupted and you are unable to maintain an even clay moisture, cover projections temporarily with strips of thin plastic sheeting until you can give them attention again. Many a fine piece has been ruined in the kiln because a handle or other part was allowed to dry too fast and the crack went unnoticed.

Pyrometric Cones*

Because of the high temperatures involved in firing a kiln load of ceramic ware, some safe dependable way must be used to determine the progress of the firing. Heat treatment is checked in the kiln by the use of slender triangular clay cones, compounded to soften and bend at specified temperatures. Such a cone is set in a holder and positioned in the kiln so the craftsman can observe it through a peephole while the kiln fires. The appropriate cone will bend when the clay objects have received the indicated combination of time and temperature necessary for maturing the ware. These cones are so commonly used that a craftsman identifies his clays and glazes by referring to the number of the cone that softens and bends halfway over in firing, when his specific materials reach their maturing point, for example: cone 5 glaze, or cone 06 red clay.

Pyrometric cones come in large and small sizes. Craftsmen who use small kilns generally use the small cones, which are about 1⅛ inch high. Those ceramists who fire in large kilns use the larger cones, 2½ inches high, which are more easily seen against the bright kiln heat. The large cones bend a little sooner than the small ones, because of their weight and height.

Cones are numbered beginning with cone 022, the lowest indicated temperature, and progress to higher heat indication by numbering *downward* through 021, 020, on down to cone 01; from that point, numbering progresses to higher heat indication with cone 1, cone 2, upward to cone 42, the highest temperature indication. Few ceramists use temperatures above cone 12. There is considerable firing temperature range in clays. It is well for the beginner to use commercial clay compounded to mature at a specified temperature, rather than to try to compound a clay with unknown characteristics.

Pyrometric cones are inserted into commercially made plaques or handmade pats of grogged clay. They are positioned at an angle of about 8° from vertical so they will bend, but not slump, which they might do if positioned exactly vertical. The general practice is to use three cones in a pat. One is a cone that will bend at the clay's maturing temperature. It is flanked by a cone one step higher in number and a cone one step lower in number; these last two cones are warning indicators. The bending of the first cone indicates that the correct firing cone will soon bend. If all three cones have bent, you have waited a little too long to shut down the kiln. Although your kiln may be

---

* For temperature equivalents of pyrometric cones, see page 109.

equipped with a pyrometer, cones not only indicate the combined effects of time and temperature but also show heat distribution throughout the kiln. Temperature is rarely uniform in all parts of a hot kiln. It is wise to distribute several pats inside the kiln to keep tab on heat fluctuation. While you are loading the kiln, it is easy to place them near the back, in a corner, on each shelf, or any other doubtful area; and of course one is set into the center of the kiln in line with the peephole so firing progress can be checked. When the kiln has cooled and is unloaded, the cones can be studied to see where heat was uneven. In future firings, objects can be positioned according to the most suitable heat distribution.

TEMPERATURE EQUIVALENTS FOR ORTON STANDARD PYROMETRIC CONES   *(As determined at the National Bureau of Standards)*

CONE NUMBER	LARGE CONES		SMALL CONES	
	150°C.*	270°F.*	300°C.*	540°F.*
022	600°C.	1112°F.	630°C. a	1165°F.a
021	614	1137	643	1189
020	635	1175	666	1231
019	683	1261	723	1333
018	717	1323	752	1386
017	747	1377	784	1443
016	792	1458	825	1517
015	804	1479	843	1549
014	838	1540	870 a	1596
013	852	1566	880 a	1615
012	884	1623	900 a	1650
011	894	1641	915 a	1680
010	894	1641	919	1686
09	923	1693	955	1751
08	955	1751	983	1801
07	984	1803	1008	1846
06	999	1830	1023	1873
05	1046	1915	1062	1944
04	1060	1940	1098	2008
03	1101	2014	1131	2068
02	1120	2048	1148	2098
01	1137	2079	1178	2152
1	1154	2109	1179	2154
2	1162	2124	1179	2154
3	1168	2134	1196	2185
4	1186	2167	1209	2208
5	1196	2185	1221	2230
6	1222	2232	1255	2291
7	1240	2264	1264	2307
8	1263	2305	1300	2372
9	1280	2336	1317	2403
10	1305	2381	1330	2426
11	1315	2399	1336	2437
12	1326	2419	1355	2471

* Temperature rise per hour.
a. These six temperatures are approximate.

Pyrometric Cone Chart by courtesy of the Edward Orton Jr. Ceramic Foundation of Columbus, Ohio.

Kiln Furniture

Shelves and half shelves are spaced with posts. These hard fire-clay supports are constructed so two or three can be combined into varying heights. Supports should be placed under the center as well as beneath edges of large shelves to deter warpage. If a shelf does warp slightly, it can be leveled with a wad of high-firing clay pressed between the "short" posts and the shelf. Clay wads must be dried before firing begins. If you make your own clay cone pats, be sure to dry them also, before the kiln is turned on.

All sorts of stilts and firing racks are available for supporting glazed ware in the kiln. Examine these aids at your local ceramics supply store to select only those items which serve your actual needs. You will soon learn just what helps you need as your work progresses and expands. You may decide to make many of your own tools.

Kiln Wash

Kiln shelves are given at least three coats of kiln wash before they are used for the first time. Then if glaze drips onto the shelf, it is scraped away easily and the surface is patched with more kiln wash. Mix dry kiln wash powder with water to the consistency of thin cream. First brush the shelf generously with water. Then with quick long strokes, brush on wash in one direction until the top of the shelf is covered. Load the brush again and apply a second coat in a crosswise direction. Apply the third coat crosswise to the second coat. It is important to let the shelf dry slowly for two or three days. The first time the shelf is heated, it should be at a low heat which is raised very gradually.

Dried kiln wash particles, crumbs of fire-brick, or flecks of glaze should be kept off the elements in an electric kiln. A vacuum cleaner with a crack cleaning attachment is convenient for cleaning up stray particles in the kiln.

Stacking the Kiln

During several stages in the first (bisque) firing, clay expands and contracts. Because the body is very weak at these times and unequal strains may cause warpage, pieces should stand level on the kiln shelf. Large wide bowls with even rims are best fired upside down to prevent rim warpage. If objects are stacked inside one another, foot rims should coincide, with no more than three pieces in a stack. Small objects are placed inside larger ones, sitting level. Clay "spurs" and "plate pins" can separate stacked ware in bisque firing so heat may circulate freely. Cups are placed rim to rim or upside down, but never sitting inside other pieces at an angle. All lidded objects are bisque-fired with covers in place. Keep an inch or more between pieces to prevent development of hot spots which cause uneven firing. Objects should be two to three inches from the walls of the kiln. Fully stacked kilns heat more uniformly than nearly empty ones.

There is divided opinion about firing bisque at lower or higher temperatures than glazed ware. Some craftsmen prefer a low-fired bisque, followed by a higher glaze fire. They feel that glaze penetrates and bonds better with the body when glaze and bisque are brought to the higher temperature together. Others believe a first higher bisque temperature will show up warpage, cracks, blisters, and other imperfections before they are covered with glaze. Currently, many ceramists are using low fusing glazes over higher fired bisque stoneware because they prefer the rich colorful low-fired glazes and lusters, but they want to work with stoneware rather than earthenware.

Glaze actually melts when it is fired and it will stick to anything that touches it in the hot kiln, including loose bits of brick and other particles that may fall on it from the walls and roof of the kiln. The kiln can be vacuumed between firings to eliminate dirt and stray particles. Avoid letting glazed pieces touch, or they will stick together. To protect kiln shelves from drippings of melted glaze, brush shelves with a coat of kiln wash between each firing. Kiln wash may be bought, or it can be made from equal parts of flint and kaolin or china clay. Drops of hardened glaze are easily scraped from shelves which have been treated with kiln wash, dissolved in water to cream consistency.

The Firing Schedule

Let us assume your unfired ceramic ware is well constructed, completely dried, and adequately stacked in the kiln ready for its first, or bisque, firing. Cones are all placed; and it is time to turn on the kiln. Although the clay is bone dry, it contains atmospheric moisture which is always present in a room and in the walls of a cold kiln. The atmospheric moisture must be driven off *slowly* at very low heat. This process is called "water-smoking." Turn the kiln burners to the lowest heat. The kiln door is left open a crack and peephole plugs are removed. Resist any temptation to hasten the firing period.

If your kiln is equipped with a pyrometer, which is an actual heat indicator, you can watch the exact hourly rate of increase in temperature. Jotting down hourly temperatures is very helpful if you want to analyze your firing results. Try to keep the temperature rising at a slow even rate. Large kilns heat gradually when they are turned low. Small electric kilns tend to heat more rapidly, even at "low." To slow the heat rise in a small kiln, leave the door cracked and peepholes open the first hour. After the first hour, they can be closed at half-hour intervals. Because the water-smoking period is a danger period for all ware, it must proceed slowly. A fully loaded kiln fires best if heat is raised only 50° F. an hour during early firing stages. Many ceramists heat-soak ware all night at stationary low heat. It may take several days to fire a full load of sculpture in a large kiln. If by now it seems that unusual stress is placed on slow

firing, you will begin to realize its importance.

Between 350° F. and 400° F. it may be assumed that atmospheric moisture has left the clay. If you are keeping track of the rate of increase in temperature, as soon as the temperature slows its rate of rise, turn the burners on medium heat, but keep the rate of rise even. Sometimes the burners are turned back to low for a short time if the heat rises too rapidly. Between 950° F. and 1300° F. chemically combined moisture, resulting from a molecular change in the structure of the clay, begins to evaporate. During this period a peephole should be open so escaping moisture can leave the kiln. Because the structure of the clay is weakened during these periods of physical change, the rise in temperature should continue to be slow and even. At 1600° F. there is a critical 15 percent change in the clay. After that the heat rise may be increased slightly. Between 1750° F. and 1850° F., alumina and silica in earthenware combine to form interlocking crystals called *mullite;* the clay becomes dense. If this stage is not reached, complete vitrification does not take place. With a larger amount of the refractory alumina in stoneware, the silica fills all open spaces in a dense vitrification at 2300° F. If your kiln has no pyrometer, turn up the burners at intervals of two to four hours, depending upon your kiln size and load.

During the firing process, clayware shrinks; there is less shrinkage in a body high in grog content, but it may be less waterproof due to increased porosity. Lack of uniformity in the pressure put on clay when ware is formed may cause uneven shrinkage during the firing, with consequent warpage. Sculpture, with its variation in wall thickness, must be supported by props of unfired clay to prevent slumping and deter uneven shrinkage and warping. The props must be identical to the clay of the ware. They may be rolled in flint to guard against adhering to the shelves when the kiln is fired.

When bending cones indicate bisque temperature has been attained, the kiln is shut down.

KILN STACKING

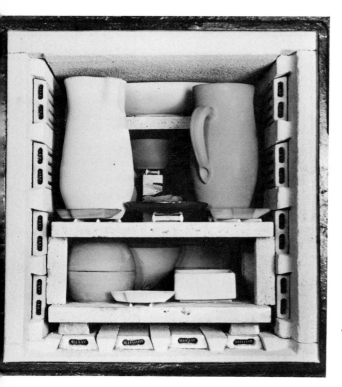

Fuel-burning kilns should be turned off and drafts closed to keep cool air from being drawn into the kiln. Temperatures in small electric kilns tend to cool too fast. Some mat glazes are shiny if they have cooled too rapidly. Small kilns should be stepped down to medium heat, then low heat, before the kiln is shut off. Large kilns are shut off when cooling begins. A kiln should take at least as long to cool as it did to heat, preferably longer. Let it cool to 200° F. before you open it. If it is opened too soon, pieces can crack, and sides and the roof of the kiln may be damaged. Because cones are compounded to bend at specified temperatures *and* rate of heat increase, an unusually slow firing may result in vitrification and the bending of cones somewhat earlier than expected. If your kiln is equipped with a pyrometer, this will be apparent. However, it may be assumed that the ware is mature when the cones bend.

This well-stacked kiln shows the use of clay spurs, stilts, and plate pins.
Courtesy American Art Clay Company.

Cutaway side view. Shelves and half shelves are supported by insulation brick posts.
Courtesy American Art Clay Company.

SECTION 3

CERAMIC DESIGN
AND DECORATION

*The innate harmony of an art object is established by certain truths which
have stood the test of time. Whether a form is severely modern in concept
or has classic design and structural overtones, basic precepts not fully
comprehended will establish some work to have lasting beauty and
acceptance, while other work may capture momentary spectacular
attention, then fade into obscurity.*

—Frank Lloyd Wright

As the craftsman studies his amorphous lump
of clay, he is aware that he must do something
with it. His fond hope is that whatever he
achieves will be acceptable to others as well as
to himself, for true artistic realization is
achieved when the inner conviction and emotional response of both the artist and the viewer
are in harmony. Because design is so intensely
personal, the following discussion is intended
only as a guideline for the sincere craftsman
who is searching for a base or starting point
from which to develop his designs. Experience
in handling clay should eventually overcome the
problem of discovering ideas for design in form
and surface enrichment. Observation, practice,
perseverance, and the casting away of precon-
ceived notions will result in ability to express
oneself in ceramic clay. It is advisable to form

the habit of carrying a notebook and pencil so you can jot down ideas that occur to you before they slip away and are lost to memory.

Some craftsmen search for inspiration in geometric forms or in man-made objects such as patterns created by machinery, scaffolding, city skylines, assemblages of pipe, and other groupings. Others may find a continuing source of inspiration in natural objects. A sense of the organic is indispensable to the artist-craftsman. The inexhaustible phenomena of nature, from tiny seedpods to mountain synclines, are everywhere around us in an incredible richness of pattern and form.

Through a serious study of many natural objects, certain subtle truths become evident. Although no form in nature is exactly like another, the discerning eye begins to recognize similarities as well as variations. The object that first attracts our attention in nature (and in art) has a dominant feature. It may be an unusual shape, a bright color or combination of colors, or a striking contrast of textures. There will be one or more secondary features relating in a lesser degree to the chief focus of our interest. Impelled to a closer inspection, we discover small interesting details and rhythms, revealing

in all their subtle variations repetitions of the dominant theme. All these truths, evident in nature's impressive designing, may also be applied to successful ceramic design, both in form and decoration.

An object made of clay offers an impelling invitation to surface enrichment. Its purpose is to enhance the form so the two make a unified convincing whole rather than a static shape with decoration imposed upon it. Successful treatment echoes or complements the form. Surface textures are subtle and inviting or boldly vigorous when they sometimes suggest and other times emphasize a configuration. Arrangements of patterns and colors often repeat illusory fragments of details of the form. On the tactile surface of a well-conceived ceramic object, these abstractions or echoes of reality make convincing design. The fusion of the individual's imagination, ideas inspired from external experiences, and the nature of his material becomes that spontaneous personal expression we call "creativeness." It is helpful to keep in mind some specific ways in which we may attain the results toward which we strive. It is with this objective in mind that the following "hints" are offered:

Vase. Elly Kuch, West Germany. Gray stoneware with white glazes. 15½" high. This strong form shows complete integration between form and surface treatment. Courtesy of the artist. Photo by Kuch.

Effects are heightened by the impact of such contrasts as textured areas positioned against smooth areas, light colors dramatized by dark colors, cool colors emphasized by warm hues, and many small elements balanced by a few well-placed large ones.

Although large scale is more dynamic than small and tight, if a design seems too big and empty, it can be broken up, while chief shapes are retained.

Too many similar units make for dullness; vary the width and length of lines and the size and shape of masses and spaces.

It may be confusing if lines and masses are too equally balanced; for more exciting results, one or the other will predominate.

Pattern on a surface is effective when it relates to and enhances the form. A single potent line can give movement and emphasis to an otherwise static shape.

Variations and repetitions of the dominant theme can be realized in the design of spouts, handles, lids, knobs, and surface patterns or textures.

Beverage dispenser. John Stephenson. Slab construction. Green and brown glaze. 27" high, 10" x 11" wide. Courtesy of the artist.

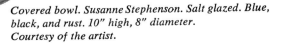

Covered bowl. Susanne Stephenson. Salt glazed. Blue, black, and rust. 10" high, 8" diameter. Courtesy of the artist.

Bottle with stopper. Leza McVey. 23" high. Courtesy of the Butler Institute of American Art.

Covered jar. Peggy Wickham. Wheel-thrown stoneware. Cone 10. Copper red and green. 12" high. Courtesy of the artist.

Luster Glazed Porcelain Domes. Susanne Stephenson.

Vase. Edwin Scheier.

Gilded Ice Bucket. Tyrone Larson.

**JUMPIN' AT THE MOON LODGE.
Michael Frimkess.**

Salt Glazed Stoneware. Donald Pilcher.

STRATA POT. Julie Larson.

Interior Wall. Nicholas Vergette.

WITCHES GRASS. *Raymond Grimm. Welded steel and stoneware. Blue and green copper oxidation glaze. 3'10" x 1'10". Courtesy of the artist.*

Vase. Petr Svoboda, Czechoslovakia. A single potent line gives movement and emphasis. 11" high. Courtesy of the artist.

Covered jar. Thomas Shafer. White glaze with blue, brown, and orange decoration. Slab built, with thrown top. Cone 10. Courtesy of the artist.

TEXTURING AND IMPRESSING

Because of its unique plastic quality, moist clay can be impressed and textured to achieve countless exciting effects. Relief is applied to the soft clay surface of ceramic objects with a variety of scratching tools, with imprinted or pressed objects, and by manipulation of the craftsman's fingers. Carved clay or plaster stamps and small texturing wheels are commonly used to press patterns into clay to extend or emphasize the design of the object. Combustible materials pressed or rolled into the surface of moist clay will burn away in the hot kiln, leaving unusual textural effects. Cereal grains, wild bird seed, sawdust, grasses, and even an arrangement of small dried weeds are some possibilities of rolled-in materials which vanish in the kiln and leave organic relief patterns. Almost any found objects that have surface texture offer possibilities for creating designs in moist clay. By pressing lightly or firmly or in a combination of both, you may achieve great variety of treatment. Moist clay slabs can be textured before they are formed into objects; or the clay form is frequently made first, then while the clay is still pliable, texture is pressed into it. This last procedure requires a firmer pressure to make an imprint. Any kind of soft pad or wad of paper toweling is pressed against the clay from the back to brace it and prevent distortion of the moist clay form.

Some unusual texturing materials are discarded news mats cast in plaster, old wooden wallpaper or fabric printing blocks and linoleum and woodcuts used in making art prints. To obtain discarded news mats, it is suggested that you contact someone in the composing room of a newspaper and ask that a few of the more interesting mats be saved for you. They are discarded daily. Cartoons, advertisements with illustrations, and interesting headlines about subjects of current interest all have design possibilities when they are used individually or collectively as a clay collage. It should be noted that a news mat pressed directly into clay will appear in reverse. If you want to print readable text, the mat must first be cast in either clay or plaster to make a negative mold. (See Press Molds.)

Old wooden printing blocks can frequently be obtained from stores that sell wares from the Orient. Although many of these old blocks are damaged or have patterns that are not useful to the craftsman, by careful selection you will find undamaged ones with delightful allover textural patterns or reliefs of exotic birds, animals, marine life, and others. These discarded blocks have been used many times with different colors of fabric inks. They are usually covered with layers of dried inks that must be removed. This stripping can be done by dousing the blocks with turpentine to loosen the ink. Let them soak awhile, then wipe off as much loosened ink as possible with old rags. After two or three dousings and wipings, most of the ink will have loosened and can be scrubbed away with a stiff brush and scouring powder. Press the cleaned block in scrap clay to test whether it is clean.

A finger can be dipped into engobe each time before impressing texture.

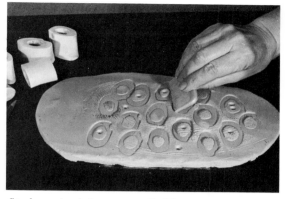

Steak or shank bones are all different. Impressions from shank bones and a pencil eraser are knit together with combing texture.

Heavy iron-oxide wash is rubbed off relief areas.

For deep texturing, an old wooden fabric-printing block is pounded into a clay slab.

Carved or intaglio-cut plaster stamps are made from plaster forms poured into small paper cups. When the plaster has set, peel off the paper cup.

Impressions from an old stylized-dragon printing block.

While the plaster is still fresh, cut a design into it with a pencil. The first pressing will pick up plaster scraps so it must be discarded.

Designs made from cut stamps and press molds.

Clay is cut around a medallion and pressed into its back to hold the medal firm against a Formica board.

OIRAN. *Kimpei Nakamura. Brown and yellow ash glaze. Courtesy* Ceramics Monthly.

A clay wall is built around each object.

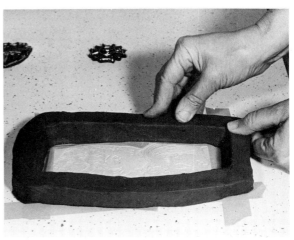

A clay wall is formed around the news mat of an advertisement illustration. Cartoons also make excellent decorative devices.

Bottle. Verne Funk. Texture applied in the glaze. Courtesy Ceramics Monthly.

Bottle. Thomas Shafer. Slab built, with thrown top. Stamped decoration and finger-pressed texture where slabs join. Unglazed, stained with iron oxide. 25" high. Courtesy of the artist.

Mix enough plaster to make several molds.

Press the clay filled side against a larger clay wad.

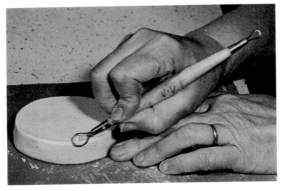

All the edges of press molds are smoothed and the sides are cleaned up.

Pressings such as this can be applied to large forms for decorative details. Press molds can be made from clay instead of plaster. The clay mold should be fired.

Clay backing is dug from the molds and the medallions are removed with a pointed tool.

Clay is rolled over the cast of a news mat for the most distinct impressions.

Press clay into the medallion cavity and discard the first pressing, which will have specks of plaster in it. Then press more clay into the form.

To bring out the design, brush or spray a metal oxide over the fired impression, then rub it off the high spots.

A red clay pinched form was beaten with a piece of bent coat hanger. White speckled glaze applied thickly at the rim ran down clay channels during glaze fire.

Decorative clay texture wheels and stamps are fired.

Lamp base. Joanna Price. Coloring was sprayed, then rubbed.

This large pinched footed form has texture applied by beating with a wire brush. Made by Maurice Rothenberg.

CARVED DESIGNS

Clay for carving must be firm but moist. If it is too dry and hard, it may crumble, crack, or flake off when it is cut. A knife used for cutting completely through the walls of a clay form must be sharp and pointed. When a design has been drawn into the clay with a pointed tool, the sharp cutting knife is pressed carefully through the moist *firm* clay along the design lines. To deter warpage, cutout sections are left in place until the clay will hold its shape without sagging. Then the pieces are pushed gently through the clay wall. If they seem to stick, retrace the cuts with the sharp pointed knife before pushing them completely free of the clay wall.

Clay walls of a form that will be carved in relief must be thick. If the shape is a thrown form, test the thickness by piercing the wall with a sharp pin while the clay is still soft. For relief carving, clay must be very firm or leather hard so the carving tool does not push the wall in instead of carving it. Draw the design directly on the firm clay. A turning tool with a sharp cutting edge is a good carving tool. Use the square end of the blade to cut clay away from the design edges, then cut or scrape the remainder of the background. It may be advisable to cut shallowly at first, then deeper as you gain experience. The gouge marks can make an interesting texture, especially if they are small and rhythmical. A raised design can be further enhanced with glazes, either on the background or on relief surfaces.

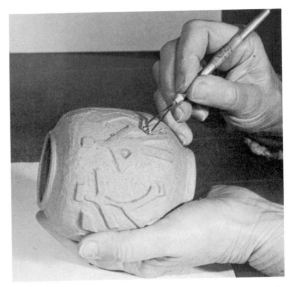

A design is drawn on the leather-hard clay of a thick walled thrown form. Then the background is carved away, leaving the design in relief.

Dark green glaze is brushed over the textured background, leaving the figures unglazed.

RARE BIRD. *M. E. Goslee. Carved sculpture. Courtesy of the Butler Institute of American Art.*

Vase. Norman Schulman. Blue carved stoneware. 15" high. Courtesy of the Butler Institute of American Art.

Candle lanterns. Gail Kristensen. Wheel thrown, distorted and carved. Stoneware clay with heavy manganese dioxide wedged in. 10" to 5" in height. Courtesy of the artist.

THE VERSATILE PATTERN PADDLE

Large or small wooden paddles carved with indented linear patterns made with a table saw or routing tool will form raised line designs when they are paddled smartly against soft clay. They may be used for an allover texture or repetitive pictorial designs, according to the way they are cut and paddled. The paddles should be made from solid wood rather than from plywood; moisture in the clay may cause plywood to separate into thin warped layers of wood. Hard pine, maple, or birch are some woods that can make serviceable paddles. All sorts of variations are achieved with only a few paddles. The clay may be smacked lightly in some areas and more sharply in others; one design laid over another is effective; or areas can be blocked off with a frisket to achieve plain shapes against textured backgrounds. The clay object may be formed first, then paddled, or slabs of clay may be paddle-textured before they are assembled.

Texturing with Grog

The addition of grog to clay produces an assortment of textures and enhances the structure of the finished objects. When grog is wedged into clay unevenly, it produces a scattering of thick and thin speckled areas. Some granular manganese wedged into clay unevenly along with grog produces a subtle organic effect when it is fired. Grog can be pressed, scraped, and manipulated into the moist surface of a completed object.

Wooden paddles carved with a table saw and routing tools make spectacular paddles, endlessly different.

Apply the paddles in different directions.

After the slab is textured, it can be stretched. The textured slabs are used for assemblages and collages.

To paddle a rounded form as it is constructed, brace the clay against paddling. Any kind of pad will work. When paddling is completed, whack the form back into shape.

A linoleum-cut pattern on the right. Plaster mold made from it on the left. Linoleum is not porous enough to use directly against clay. Linocut by Joan Martin.

The mold was stamped once on the clay tile to the left. A varied and interesting texture is made by stamping the plaster mold in several directions on the clay to the right.

CLAY APPLIQUÉ*

Thin clay slabs applied to a thicker slab or other clay form make a design in shallow relief. The demonstration project is a clay appliqué panel. Cut out a cardboard replica of the planned panel shape; then cut a replica of the thinner slab that will be applied to the panel. With a modeling tool or knife, cut around the base cardboard pattern on a slab of grogged sculpture clay about ½ inch thick. Cut out the shape that will be applied from a thinner slab between ¼ inch and ⅛ inch thick. To mark the exact location for the clay design to be applied, gently press the *cardboard* pattern of the applied shape into the base slab. Otherwise the thin clay appliqué may stretch out of shape as you are attempting to position it. With this pre-marking, it can be quickly and accurately placed.

Slip made of the same clay is brushed over the pattern area, and the clay appliqué is pressed onto the slab base. The edges of the appliqué are softly tooled in so it merges with the base. Additional tooling over the applied clay shape is free and unstudied to give a sculptural quality to the design. The completed panel is dried slowly between several layers of newspaper to deter warpage. It is fired on stilts so that air may circulate freely.

If the piece will be glazed, plunge it into water for a thorough wetting before you brush on the glaze. It will prevent the very porous bisque from unevenly "grabbing" the glaze before it can be brushed smooth. Apply two or three thin coats of glaze crosswise to each preceding coat, dry thoroughly, and fire to the recommended glaze temperature. Unglazed bisque may be waxed or stained if preferred.

There are many variations of clay appliqué, involving the use of clay slabs, coils, and rolls of clay, which are applied in some manner to a larger clay surface.

* From an article by Polly and Maurice Rothenberg, which appeared in *Design* magazine.

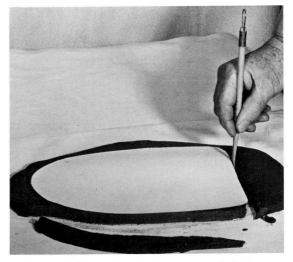

With a modeling tool or knife, cut around the base pattern on a slab of grogged sculpture clay.

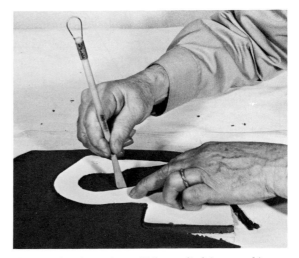

Cut out the shape that will be applied from a thinner slab.

Clay slip is brushed over the pattern area.

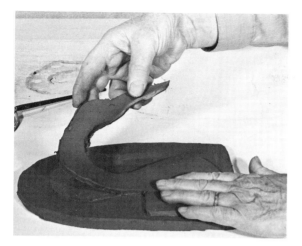

The clay appliqué is pressed onto the slab base.

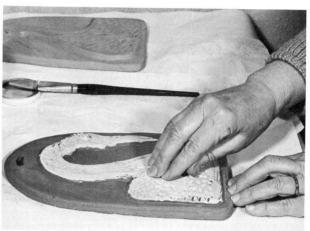

Brushed glaze is rubbed in for better bonding with the clay.

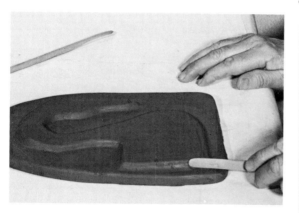

The edges of the appliqué are tooled so it merges with the background.

The applied forms are glazed in transparent brown. The red clay background is unglazed. Project by Maurice Rothenberg.

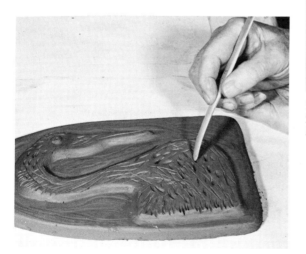

Tooling over the applied shape is free and unstudied.

Vase. Edwin Scheier. Thrown form. The background was pushed out while the form was still soft (repoussé). Appliqué and sgraffito design. Black, gold, and blue. 22½" x 15". Courtesy of the artist.

SPINEY FORM. Anne Van Kleeck. Applied clay spines. Green glaze, 13½" high. Courtesy of the Butler Institute of American Art.

Teapot. Miron Webster. Applied and incised decoration. Glazed inside, stained outside. Approximately 9" high.

Edwin and Mary Scheier inspect a museum piece in their New Hampshire studio.

Slab floor vase. John Stephenson. Applied slabs with newsprint mat impressions. 15" x 13" x 18". Black and white with gold luster. Mr. Stephenson is professor of Art at the University of Michigan, Ann Arbor. Courtesy of the artist.

CLAY CLOISONNÉ

A design involving the use of tiny flat square coils to make little enclosures for holding glazes is called *cloisonné*. Cut a panel of red grogged clay. A square thick coil (½ inch) can be applied to the edge for a raised rim, or it can be omitted if you prefer a rimless version. The background is sponged lightly to bring grog to the surface for texture. Draw a design composed of many little enclosed spaces by marking directly into the moist clay with a pencil. Slip is brushed over the penciled lines just before tiny square coils are applied to them. All the little enclosures must be sealed shut so glaze does not leak out when fired. If the work seems to dry, keep it moist by spraying it. When the panel has been dried and bisque fired, fill all the small enclosures to the top with colored glazes. When the glaze is completely dry, fire to cone 06.

Weld a tiny coil into the juncture angle between base and rim.

The right angled end of a wooden rib straightens and smooths the panel's outside edge.

A ½-inch-thick square coil is pressed firmly along the scored edge of a thick oval clay base.

Tiny moist square coils are cut from a thin slab and applied immediately over the penciled design lines that are moistened with slip.

A bent piece of cardboard incises curved cross-hatching into the background.

Cloisons are filled completely with glazes from a slip trailer.

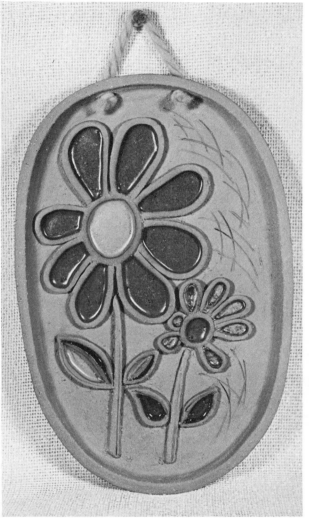

Colors are blue, turquoise, olive green, and light green on an unglazed red clay background.

Bottle. Thomas Shafer. Slab built, with thrown top. 11' high. Small flat strips form miniature enclosures. Fired unglazed to cone 10. Low-temperature glazes in bright colors are applied in small areas like cloisonné, fired to cone 08. Courtesy of the artist.

TOOLED TEXTURE

Tooled patterns are scored in soft clay. Although any kind of bluntly pointed objects may be used to score the clay, wooden modeling tools are handy and are available in a variety of sizes and shapes. Because the clay is soft, mistakes are quickly erased just by smoothing out the clay and starting over. Intricate patterns formed of thin lines or bold, casual, freely drawn sketches are appropriate for this method. Fine regular scorings make interesting background texture around applied clay shapes.

The clay disks must be assembled and dried directly on the kiln shelf. It is almost impossible to transport the assemblage before it is fired, without its falling apart.

Clay "cookies" are cut from red clay with assorted sizes of tin cans. Each clay disk is scored with modeling tools, bottle tops, combings, or pressings.

Overlapping backs of clay disks are scored, moistened, then pressed firmly together.

The completed unglazed collage is hung with a leather thong. Texture could be further emphasized by oxide wash rubbing.

A tooled stoneware panel. Joanna Price.

Slab bottle. Petr Svoboda. Textured and incised. 7" high. Courtesy of the artist.

Stoneware bowl. Donald Schaumburg. Tooled and textured with fingers. Pushed out from the inside. Yellow glaze over a brown body. Mr. Schaumburg teaches at Arizona State University at Tempe. Courtesy of the artist.

Seedpod vase. Miron Webster. Stoneware, cone 10. Scored and finger impressed. Stained. 12" high. Courtesy of the artist.

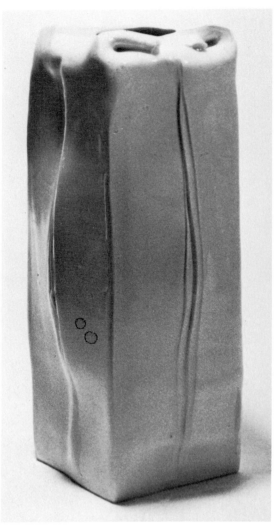

Porcelain vessel. Kurt and Gerda Spurey.
Slab built, distorted, and scored. Pure white, 15½" high.
Courtesy of the artists.

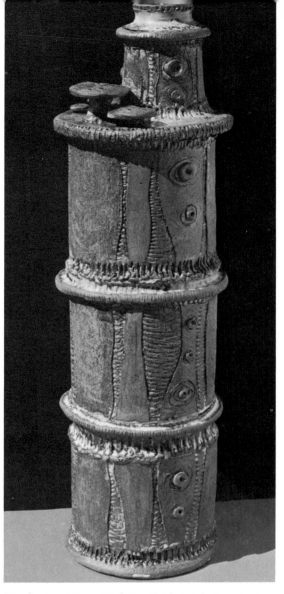

Weed vase. Miron Webster. Sculptured stoneware,
cone 10 reduction fired. Applied clay, scored, and
stained. 24" high. Courtesy of the artist.

Vase. Miron Webster. Stoneware. Clay applied and
tooled heavily. Partly stained exterior, glazed interior.
10" high. Courtesy of the artist.

Candleholders. Miron Webster. Red stoneware, cone 10 reduction. Applied, impressed, and tooled design. 11″ high. Stained clay. Courtesy of the artist.

Seedpod vase. Miron Webster. Stoneware, reduced. Applied clay, heavily tooled and impressed. Mat glaze. 18″ high. Courtesy of the artist.

Bowl. Miron Webster. Stoneware. Design was made with a carved brick, impressed; then clay was distorted with the fingers. Courtesy of the artist.

CLAY INLAY

Some natural clays and clay bodies are distinguished by their subtle and interesting colors. When they are inlaid in clays of contrasting color, they make effective decorative devices. A project with a clay inlay design should be made with clays of similar texture and firing temperatures so that shrinkage and maturing temperatures are compatible. Otherwise the inlaid portion will separate from the main body of the form when it is dried and fired.

Because clays change color when they are fired, it is advisable to fire small samples of each different clay before you begin an important inlay project. To keep all the clays for the project of even moisture content, wedge portions of each clay and wrap them in plastic. While you work, protect the various clays from making smudges of color on one another. Clean your hands frequently to keep clay colors clean and well defined.

ROLLED CLAY INLAY

The tiny coil is formed of moist contrasting color clay.

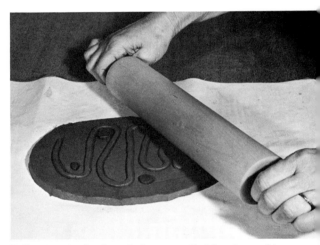

Balls of a third color of clay are rolled in along with the coiled pattern.

A clay oval is cut out around a plaster drape mold, leaving plenty of space for draping.

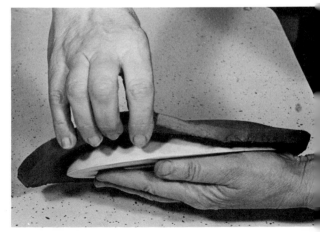

The pressed clay oval is positioned over the plaster mold; make sure the design does not extend beyond the mold.

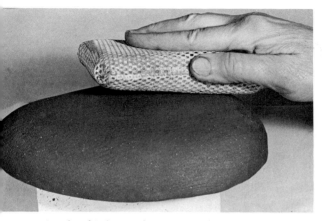

A nylon kitchen pad textures and pats the clay to fit. It is supported on a Styrofoam block for easy trimming.

Flattened clay ball feet are applied over scored and moistened spots.

When the form has been fired, the different clays make effective contrast.

CUT CLAY INLAY

Practice exercise: A clay shape is cut from a textured brown clay slab.

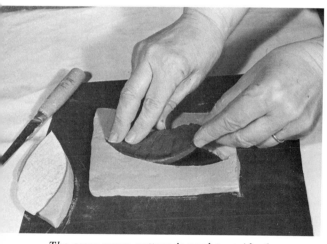

The same paper pattern is used to guide the duplication of a similar shaped opening in lighter clay. Edges of the dark clay insert are moistened before it is fitted carefully into the opening.

CLAY OVERLAY AND INLAY SLAB FORM

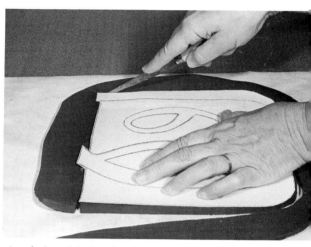

A red clay slab for the object's front panel is cut around a pattern.

Lines for the thinner slab overlay design are traced into the panel to facilitate positioning of the applied shapes.

The bowl of the pedestal form, assembled from mitered-edge slabs, is reinforced with small clay coils worked into the corners.

Tiny coils are worked into the corners with a decorative tooling.

Location for the tall slab pedestal is scored and slipped. Notice the front of the form is positioned over the table edge as protection for the front-panel extensions.

The three different clay colors will show more contrast when the leather-hard object is dried and fired.

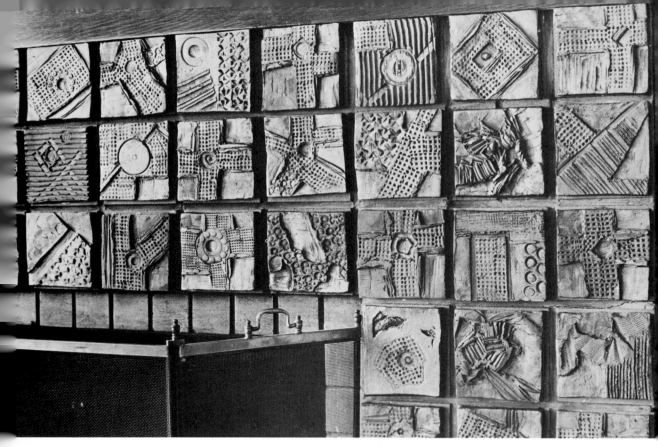

Ceramic relief mural. Michi Zimmerman. 69 tiles, 6½″ x 6½″ x 2″. Stoneware with iron oxide stain. Mounted with epoxy tile cement. Courtesy of the artist.

Weed container. Michi Zimmerman. White slip with black oxide decoration. 8″ diameter by 2½″ thick. Cone 6. Courtesy of the artist.

Compote. Miska Petersham. Courtesy of the Butler Institute of American Art.

Slab covered jar. Miron Webster. Applied clay, heavily tooled. Light glaze brushed over raised areas. Stoneware, cone 10 reduction fired. 7" high. Courtesy of the artist.

Hanging vase. Kimpei Nakamura. Slab formed and heavily tooled. Courtesy of Ceramics Monthly.

Weed vase. Miron Webster. Slab-built stoneware. Clay overlay, scored and textured. 12" high. Courtesy of the artist.

DECORATING WITH SLIP (ENGOBES)

Slip is made from powdered clay that is available at ceramic supply stores in white and many colors. The dry slip is mixed with water to the consistency of thin paint and is easily applied with a brush. It is applied over moist firm unfired clay. Clay slip is used in countless exciting methods of decoration: painted designs, sgraffito, Mishima, wax resist, oxide coloring, and slip trailing, among the more familiar.

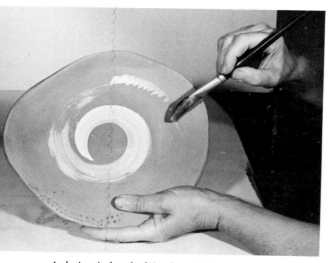

A design is brushed freely with slip over firm moist clay.

Slip Painting

Because a slip-painted design is most effective when applied freely, it is advisable to sketch a simple idea on paper, then swing into its execution quickly and with confidence, using the sketch as a guide. Apply the design on moist, firm, unfired clay. A bamboo-handled Oriental watercolor brush or any other pointed soft brush can be used. When the piece is fired, it can be covered with a transparent glaze.

Slightly dry slip gives a rugged line, moist slip allows for a smoother effect. Scratch firmly through to the clay body. Brush it lightly with a soft brush to clean away bits of dry slip and clay. Fire before glazing.

Sgraffito

The process of cutting or scratching linear patterns through an unfired layer of slip or glaze to expose the surface beneath is called *sgraffito*. That surface may be the clay body or a fired base coat of slip. Delicate or bold spontaneous patterns are exciting when they are combined with other methods of decoration. Lines vary dramatically according to the kind of scratching tool used and degree of pressure applied, as well as whether the clay base is leather hard, dry, or fired. Lines scratched through dry slip are feathery and crisp while smoother lines are achieved by incising through moist slip.

White slip is painted over leather-hard clay to make a base for sgraffito.

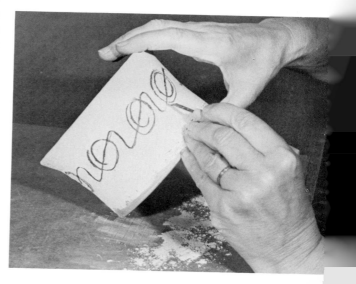

Transparent yellow majolica glaze makes the red clay a rich brown where no slip is applied and over the scratched lines.

Moist slip gives a smooth sgraffito line.

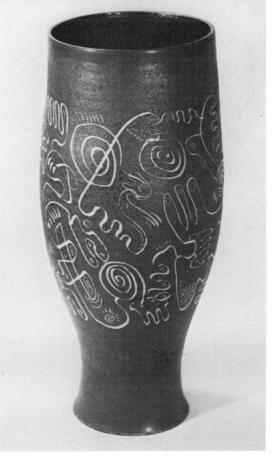

Vase. Edwin and Mary Scheier. Black metallic glaze with linear sgraffito. Courtesy of the artists.

Stoneware form. Larry Calhoun. Unglazed, with slip decoration. Courtesy of the artist.

*Stoneware form. Don Schaumburg.
Bright blue slip splotches
under bright blue glaze.
Fired to cone 10.
Courtesy of the Mathews Center,
American Collection, Arizona State
University, Tempe.*

Mishima

Mishima is a slip inlay technique of Oriental origin. A pattern is cut or scratched into leather-hard clay. The incised lines must be filled with lighter or darker slip. Cover them and the area immediately around them with a coating of slip applied with a heavily loaded small brush or a slip trailer (a plastic squeeze bottle with a pointed top). When the slip is dry, the surface is scraped carefully. Only the incised design remains filled with slip.

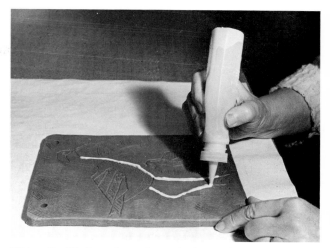

White slip fills in and overflows the line indentations.

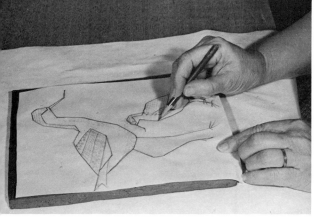

A line drawing is traced over the sketch to score the clay beneath.

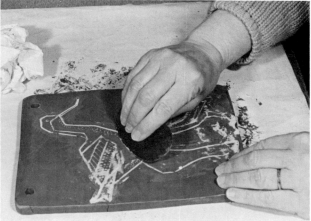

A metal scraper removes excess slip, leaving only the filled lines.

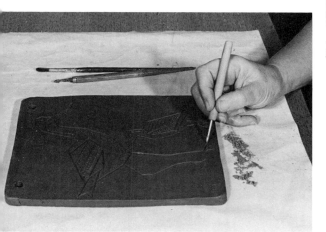

The traced design is cut deeply with a sgraffito tool.

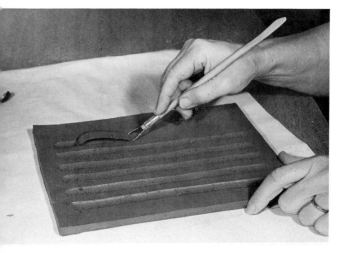

Grooves are cut into the back of the tile to speed drying. To prevent warpage, dry tiles between sheets of newspaper, and stilt the tiles in the kiln.

The completed panel is unglazed.

Slip trailing

Slip is trailed by squeezing very thick slip through a plastic slip trailer or any plastic bottle, such as a mustard dispenser, which has a pointed cap with a hole in the top. When you lay down a line of trailed slip, do not pause uncertainly or a thick dot will form. Slip is trailed on firm moist clay. If the clay is too dry, the slip may crack loose as it dries.

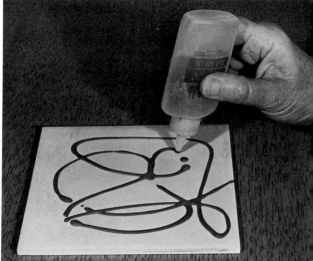

Slip is trailed from a plastic squeeze bottle. It must be applied to moist firm clay and dried slowly.

Decorating on the Wheel

For spectacular designing on shallow bowl or plate forms, fasten the plate on the throwing wheel head with a wad of clay, start the wheel at high speed, and pour small amounts of harmonizing slips or glazes on the spinning plate. Choose colors carefully. A little black and some white will sharpen the effect. Pour dark colors first. It takes a moment for the colors to start spreading. Refinements like sgraffito and spatter add to the delightful designs that are endlessly different.

Fasten a plate securely to the wheel head and turn speed to fast. Pour the first glaze near the center. After it has spread somewhat, pour a different color nearer to the plate rim.

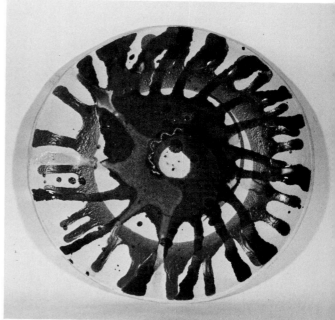

Spatter and sgraffito have been added by hand. Colors are red brown, blue green, black, and white over fired buff stoneware.

Pour some white off center before the wheel is started so it stays on one side after the wheel is turned on.

OXIDE COLORANTS

It is not necessary to use a great variety of decorating materials to create ceramics of simple and distinctive beauty, if you understand and use freely the versatile coloring oxides. A metal oxide, such as iron, cobalt, or copper, mixed with water, is brushed on a fired or unfired clay surface to give an entire range of colors according to the strength or weakness of the solution. The oxides are used in a method similar to watercolors; a thin mixture gives a light tint, a thicker solution gives dark colors or even black.

Mix a small amount of one of the oxides into a thick solution in a small container; a coaster is fine for this. Wet a small brush, dip its tip into the mixture, and apply a stroke on a white unglazed tile. Without adding more oxide, dip the brush tip into water and apply a thinner stroke to the tile. Repeat the process, making successively thinner strokes, until you have filled the tile. Fire the tile, then glaze it with a colorless transparent glaze. A thin application of glaze makes oxides bright and colorful. The completed tile will show what oxides can do as painting material.

Metal oxides may be brushed or sponged onto a fired clay surface that has strong texture to emphasize configuration. Apply a medium coat of any oxide colorant, then wipe it off the high spots. Fire to the clay's indicated temperature. It may be glazed with a transparent glaze or left unglazed. When oxides are applied to fired clay, details remain sharp; on unfired clay, the moisture smooths away sharpness of details. Coloring oxides are used like watercolors when they are painted over a fired white slip-covered clay surface.

METAL OXIDE WASHES

A heaping teaspoon of iron oxide is mixed in two cups of water for a heavy wash.

The wash is sponged over a moistened *textured clay bisque.*

The oxide is rubbed off high points with a rag.

Texture made with a piece of coral is emphasized.

Branch bottle. Gail Kristensen. Light buff clay with heavy grog. Manganese dioxide wash rubbed into the crevices to emphasize texture. Glazed top. 26" high. Courtesy of the artist.

A textured buff stoneware bisqued form is moistened, then brushed with several coats of thin iron-oxide wash to emphasize texture. When the piece is refired, the buff clay will have acquired a soft caramel color.

Umbrella holder. Gail Kristensen. Light buff stoneware. Rolled slab. Manganese dioxide outside, glazed inside. 24" high. Courtesy of the artist.

Vase. Dorothy Larson-Hotchkiss. The design was incised, then cobalt oxide rubbed in. A mat glaze overall. Courtesy of the Cooper-Hewitt Museum, Smithsonian Institution.

Vase. Larry Calhoun. Stoneware. Ash glaze with iron and cobalt oxides. 24" high. Courtesy of the artist.

METAL OXIDES

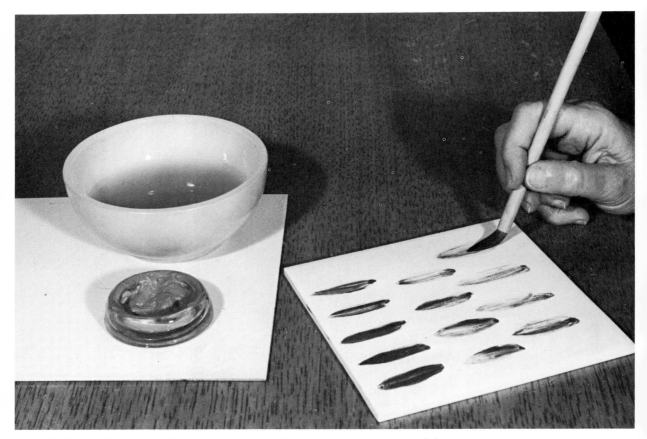

*To learn what oxides will do, make a paste of one, such as copper or cobalt.
Dip the tip of a soft pointed brush into it and make a brushstroke on a
fired white tile. Dip the brush into a little water (without adding more
oxide to the brush) and make another stroke. Make more successive strokes,
diluting each one in additional water. Fire the tile, then glaze it with clear
glaze. From this simple exercise, you will learn much about metal oxides
and carbonates. Because the coloring capacity of some of the oxides is greater
than others, it is wise to try this exercise with different ones.*

WAX RESIST AND OXIDES OVER SLIP

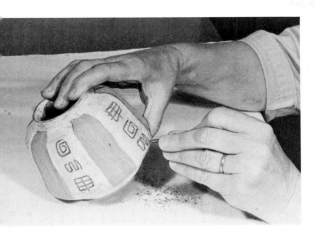

When the piece is fired, the wax burns away in the heat, leaving streaks and spots of color deposited on the white areas.

White slip panels are painted over a leather-hard clay bowl. The white panels are covered with wax resist emulsion. Line designs are scratched through to the clay.

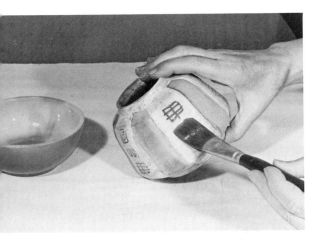

A wash of copper oxide is painted overall; the wax protects the white panels.

APPLE POT. David Black. 17" high. Wax resist and sgraffito decoration. Courtesy of the Butler Institute of American Art.

Footed bowl. Thomas Sellers. Constructed of two thrown components joined at the leather-hard stage. Wax resist, sgraffito decoration, in separate processes, over a dull orange mat glaze. Cone 04. Courtesy of the artist.

TOTEM POT. *David Black. 13½" high. Wax resist decoration. Courtesy of the Butler Institute of American Art.*

GLAZING

Care in Glaze Handling

Ceramic glazes in every conceivable color and special effect are available at ceramic supply houses. These glazes are sold dry in bulk form ready for mixing with water, or packaged in ready-to-use liquid form. The novice, eager to complete his ceramic forms and enhance them with colorful glazing, is encouraged to try these excellent ready-prepared commercial glazes. When he has acquired an understanding of the use and proper handling of glaze chemicals, he may eventually seek the experience of mixing glazes from the many glaze formulas to be found in potters' handbooks.

The formulation and calculation of glazes is a complex and specialized science. It is not a field that can be conquered by haphazard experimentation. The same common sense and care must be exercised in handling and using glazes and glaze chemicals that we employ in our contacts with other craft materials, such as volatile oils, paints, cleaning acids, and etching mordants. Some glaze chemicals, such as lead, are not safe when ingested. Not all glazes contain lead compounds; these glazes may be used freely. Certain manufacturers of commercial ceramic supplies have a line of safe leadless glazes compounded especially for use on ceramic food containers. Much glazed ceramic ware never comes in contact with food (sculpture, vases, murals, panels, and other decorative surfaces). Before using a prepared glaze for ceramic food containers, find out whether it is a guaranteed "safe" glaze by inquiring of your supplier or the glaze manufacturer. Always follow carefully the instructions and precautions that accompany ceramic materials.

Porcelain covered jar. Jack Feltman. White background with metallic gold crystals. 15" tall. Cone 10. Courtesy of the artist.

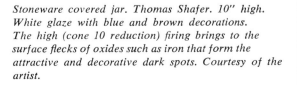

Stoneware covered jar. Thomas Shafer. 10" high. White glaze with blue and brown decorations. The high (cone 10 reduction) firing brings to the surface flecks of oxides such as iron that form the attractive and decorative dark spots. Courtesy of the artist.

Branch container. Gail Kristensen. Stoneware slab construction. 24" high. Brown clay with heavily applied semimat olive green glaze. The interior separates into compartments to allow individual placement of branches so they remain upright. Courtesy of the artist.

Certain safety measures must be followed in handling glaze materials. Keep your hands away from your face and wash them after handling either commercial glazes or individual glaze chemicals. Follow a regular schedule of keeping your work areas clean and neat by regular vacuuming instead of sweeping and stirring glaze dust into the air, where it will be drawn into the lungs. To avoid breathing toxic spray mist, *always* apply sprayed glazes in well-ventilated spray booths equipped with an exhaust fan. The kiln should be located in a separate work area or room equipped with hooded exhausts. Harmful fumes emanate from a hot kiln when some ceramic chemicals change their molecular structure and give off gas in the presence of heat. This discussion is not intended to alarm but to inform on the proper care and handling of ceramic materials. These safety measures should become just as routine as any other precautions exercised in human activities.

The Mixing and Application of Glazes

Glazes must be blended thoroughly before they are applied. If you plan to mix individual dry ingredients, using one of the many excellent glaze recipes to be found in glaze handbooks, copy the list of ingredients and place the paper near the mixing area. Lay a creased piece of paper on the gram scale, then weigh out the first ingredient. Dump it into a bowl and check it on the list. Proceed with the next ingredient, making certain you check it. It is very easy to forget where you are on the list, if you do not check each item as it is weighed. When all the ingredients have been weighed and put into the bowl, stir in enough water to make a medium thin mixture if the glaze is to be poured or dipped —a slightly thicker mix if it will be brushed. To obtain good results it is necessary to blend the glaze. If you do not have access to a ball mill, a kitchen blender will do the job very well for small batches. A blender is a handy piece of equipment for mixing ready-prepared dry glazes with water, or for remixing small amounts of lumpy or partly dried-out moist ones.

Ready-prepared moist glazes bought from reliable suppliers are usually in good condition when you receive them. Sometimes the glaze seems thick and jellylike, due to the type of binder blended into the glaze to make it more adhesive. It can still be brushed, but a little water may have to be added to the glaze (and stirred well), if pieces are to be dipped or poured. Glazes for spraying must be ground very fine. As described earlier, they must be applied in a spray booth that is adequately equipped with an exhaust fan.

Although some ceramists glaze greenware (unfired clay objects) to save the time of a second firing, there are hazards involved: greenware is very fragile and easily broken; it can absorb too much water from the wet glaze and crumble or crack. If greenware is constructed thickly, the glaze may be poured or sprayed safely. By far the most glazing is done on bisque.

Before a piece of bisque ware is glazed, sponge it off thoroughly with water to clean away dust or finger marks that may have accumulated. Low firing porous bisque should be plunged into water to add moisture to the porous clay so it will not "grab" the glaze and make a thick lumpy glaze surface. Stoneware bisque fired high should be wiped off with a damp cloth. Since it is not porous, wetting it too much may make the glaze run off the surface without covering adequately. Stoneware is frequently bisqued much lower than its temperature of maturity; then glaze and body are brought to the higher heat together. But today many craftsmen like to use the colorful and versatile glazes of lower firing temperatures, and they are bisque-firing stoneware to maturity before they glaze. Properly wetting the bisque has much to do with success in glazing. If a porous bisque piece that you are brush-glazing begins to accumulate a thick messy layer of glaze,

scrape it all off and start over; wet the ware again, more quickly this time because it already has some moisture and it might be wet too much. Only experience will guide the correct amount of moisture to be applied.

When a porous ware has been liberally soaked, it may take considerable time to dry completely. It must be thoroughly dry before it is fired. Because time is very important to the craftsman who sells much of his work, many ceramists prefer to dip their pieces dry. This must be done very quickly to get a good coverage. Do not be discouraged if your first glazed pieces are a disappointment. Start with easily made simple forms. Save your larger ones until you have glazed some test ware.

When a glaze is to be brushed, after the ware has been moistened, use a small brush to glaze intricate or partly concealed areas. Then load a larger brush and apply long even strokes that go with the longest dimension of the object. If the piece is held perpendicular over a bowl the loaded brush can be swept down over the form, letting glaze flow back into the bowl. If the glaze seems uneven or thick anyplace, it is advisable to wait until the glaze is dry, then gently stroke a finger over the dry thick spot to smooth it out, rather than try to brush it away with the wet glaze brush. Too heavy an application of glaze may cause it to run when it is fired. Sometimes this is done intentionally for a decorative effect. With experience you will be able to judge the amount of glaze to be applied.

Glazes for pouring inside bowls, bottles, pitchers, vases, and other restricted forms should be thin. Pour glaze inside, roll the piece around, and pour out the excess glaze. Widemouth forms are inverted over two long narrow sticks placed across a bowl. If the bowl is positioned on a banding wheel (bench wheel), one hand can rotate the wheel while the other hand pours glaze over the exterior surface of the form. The ware is left inverted on the sticks until the glaze loses its shine. Brush the top of the rim where it touched the sticks. Carefully wipe glaze off the foot. To glaze the exterior of a necked form, hold it by the top while you pour glaze over it; then set it down and finish glazing the top with a brush.

Small forms can be dipped into glaze with dipping tongs. Although large forms can be dipped, a deep container with a large amount of glaze is required. This may be practical where many pieces are to be covered with a limited number of glazes. When an object is dipped into glaze, if it is held upside down, air may be trapped beneath it preventing glaze from entering the interior. Sometimes the air suddenly escapes with a giant "blurp" that splashes glaze over the vicinity. It is advisable to dip the form into the glaze sideways to avoid this nuisance. The bottom surface of glazed ware should be kept clean of glaze to prevent it from sticking to the shelf when the kiln is fired. If many pieces are to be dip-glazed, to save time liquid wax can be brushed quickly over the foot or base to prevent glaze from adhering to it. Glazed ware that is covered entirely should be stilted when it is fired. Stilt marks are filed smooth.

When a glaze is fired, slow cooling of the kiln is important. If a mat glaze is shiny, it may be the kiln has cooled too fast. Small electric kilns tend to cool too rapidly if they are shut off completely. By stepping down the temperature of a small kiln, the glazed ware can cool slowly. Glazed pieces should not be placed too close together in the kiln; they may develop hot spots or shiny places where they are in proximity.

BRUSH GLAZING

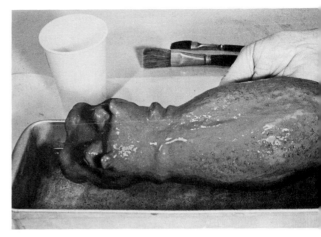

A porous bisque ware is plunged into water and immersed completely so it becomes evenly wet before glazing begins.

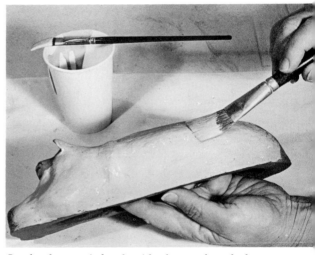

Load a large soft brush with glaze and apply long even strokes that go with the length of the form. Flow the glaze on smoothly.

The completed form cemented to a ceramic base.

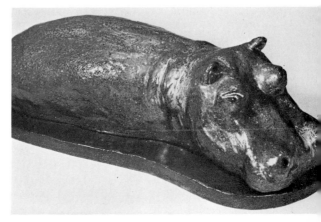

Large forms should be plunged quickly into and out of a deep container for complete immersion.

Let the glaze drain over two sticks propped over a bowl or bucket.

Pour glaze inside, roll it around, and pour it out.

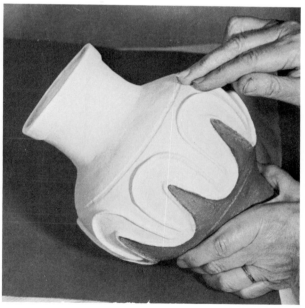

When the glaze has been brushed on, it can be rubbed in while it is still moist. Rubbing the glaze works it into the bisque and brings some of the body color into the glaze when it is fired. Rubbing a glaze is optional.

POURING AND DIPPING GLAZES

A thin glaze is poured on a form so it will flow evenly around curves.

DIPPING TONGS

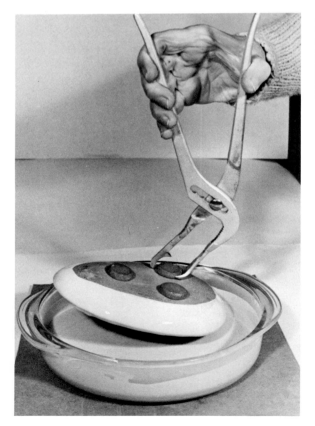

SPRAYING GLAZES

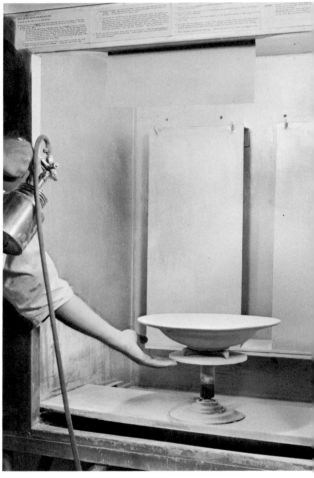

Hold the glaze gun back from the ware when you spray. If it is held too close, the glaze will puddle and run. Rotate the wheel evenly for an even coverage. Always spray glazes in a spray booth adequately equipped with an exhaust fan.

This useful and adjustable tool has pointed prongs, placed vertically on one arm, horizontally on the other, to facilitate grasping complex forms.

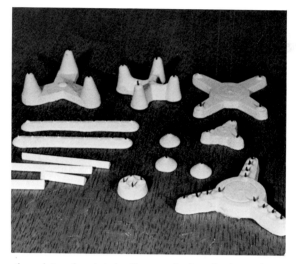

A variety of pointed stilts can be bought for stilting glazed ware in the kiln, as a precaution for protecting the kiln floor from a runny glaze.

COLORED AND METALLIC LUSTERS

Ready-prepared metallic and colored lusters are applied over glossy fired glazes. Luster will be no glossier than the glaze beneath it. Pearl or rainbow lusters applied over colored glazes give the semblance of a colored luster; over a white glaze, they resemble mother-of-pearl. A lustrous depth is attained by applying a colored luster over a glossy glaze of the same color, such as pink luster over a light pink glaze. Colored lusters applied over white give a more delicate effect. For darker color, apply two coats *with a firing between.*

To apply lusters, wipe the glazed piece with a cloth moistened in denatured alcohol or lighter fluid. Using a soft clean brush, flow on a thin translucent coating of luster. Avoid going over an area more than once. It is wise to use separate brushes for each different luster color, even though it means an investment in brushes. Because the color clings to a brush rather persistently, it is difficult to remove every vestige of luster. Clean the brush thoroughly each time it is used. If a trace of luster is accidentally smeared where it isn't wanted, it must be wiped off immediately with alcohol or lighter fluid. Use a china paint eraser to remove *fired* luster.

When luster application is completed, set the ware in a warm place overnight, such as on top a warm kiln. When it is ready to be fired, put it into the kiln with the room well ventilated. Leave the door partly open and heat turned to low so fumes from burning oils can escape. This is important, especially when a considerable area of the ware is covered with luster. The burning oils make a smoke which must escape from the kiln before it can settle on your ware. Kiln heat for lusters, cone 018 to cone 020, is too low to consume smoke. Raise the kiln heat very gradually with the kiln door open about a half inch for at least two hours. By then the fumes should be dissipated. Watch the kiln

Stoneware footed bowl. Edwin Scheier. The bowl's interior and the background around figures of Last Supper *design are decorated with sprayed glazes. Overglaze details. Courtesy of the artist.*

closely when the temperature approaches cone 020. A pyrometer is very helpful when luster is fired (approximately 1200°F.). As soon as top heat is reached, turn off the kiln completely so the luster is not held at top heat, if you want to avoid the hazard of burning it. Most lusters mature at cone 019, but some may mature at cone 020.

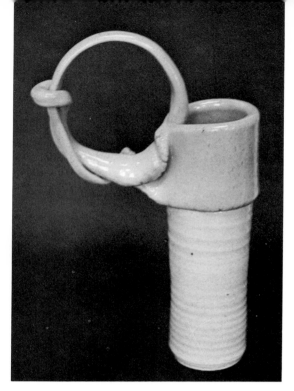

Vase. Patrick McCormick. Earthenware glazed in white with pink luster overall. 20" high. Mr. McCormick teaches at Western Washington State University. Courtesy of the artist.

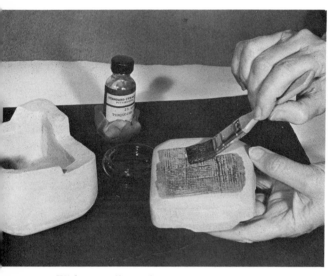

With a small soft brush, flow on a thin even coat of luster over a fired glaze.

Turquoise luster over the top of a sculptured box.

Gilded covered bowl. Julie Larson. Stoneware clay with celadon glaze, banded in platinum luster. 18" high, 15" in diameter. Courtesy of the artist.

RAMONA THE RAINMAKER. *Randall Schmidt. Stoneware clay body glazed in blue low fire glaze, then covered with mother-of-pearl luster. Top and center are of platinum luster. At top center is bright pink silicone rubber. 16" high. From the collection of Dr. and Mrs. Earl W. Linderman, Arizona. Mr. Schmidt teaches at Arizona State University at Tempe.*

ONE-OF-A-KIND CERAMICS. *Patrick McCormick. Stoneware with black and pewter luster. 36" high. Courtesy of the artist.*

DECORATING WITH LUMP ENAMEL

Enamel lumps work well on either flat or inclined surfaces. When they are applied to a vertical surface, some provision must be made to cope with possible enamel drippings. The demonstration vase was supported in the kiln on an insulation brick *narrower* than the circumference of the base of the vase. Heavy kiln wash on the kiln floor takes care of any additional dripping. With experience, very little drip will be encountered as you learn how far a given size lump will flow. Opaque enamel lumps have a thicker viscosity than transparents when they melt. On a vertical or inclined surface, lump enamel is applied by pressing it into *unfired clay.* When glaze is applied to the bisqued ware, the second firing will not damage the enamel.

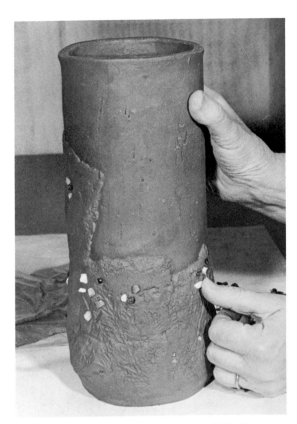

A cylindrical vase was formed over a field tile (three-inch diameter) as illustrated under Drape Molds. When the clay was firm, lumps of bright opaque enamels, the kind used in metal enameling, were pressed firmly into the applied textured red clay. When the vase was dry, it was fired to cone 06.

Dark green mat glaze was brushed over the top section of the bisque form; it was fired again to cone 06.

For another project, a clay slab was textured with a bisque texture wheel; it was cut and draped over a four-inch field tile to make a low bowl. A flat coil is tooled to the base for a foot rim.

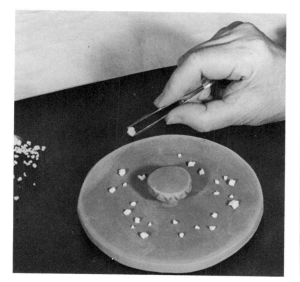

Bowl and lid are brushed with a black mat glaze. Before the glaze is fired, hard white opaque enamel lumps are positioned on the lid.

The lid was fired flat.

EFFLORESCENCE II. *Patriciu Mateescu.*

EFFLORESCENCE I. *Patriciu Mateescu, Romania. The use of lump enamel is important in the sculptural work of Mr. Mateescu. Courtesy of the artist.*

SECTION 4

CERAMIC SCULPTURE
AND ARCHITECTURE

SCULPTURE FROM
GEOMETRIC FORMS

In ceramic sculpture, forms relate to the texture, plasticity, and firing properties of the clay itself. The ability of clay to maintain a shape attained by pressure deformation makes it peculiarly adaptable to the development of open sculpture in all its variety. Space becomes a material which has the faculty of structural volume like any firm substance. Because of the disk shape of minute clay particles, compressing, compacting, and modeling these microscopic wafers into place causes them to cling closely together; the clay will hold its form around surprisingly large open spaces. Because of the peculiar firing properties of clay, sculptural forms must be made hollow. When the kiln temperature reaches the point where chemically combined moisture must make its way out of the dense clay, a large solid form would likely break apart in the kiln.

There are several methods of building a hollow structure. The most direct process is to model a solid form, then scoop out the inside clay to leave a hollow shell with even wall thickness. In small forms, the clay is scooped out from beneath. Larger sculptures may be cut apart so each portion can be hollowed, then welded together again. Sculptures can be built with clay coils. The main masses are coiled from the base upward following a penciled outline guide on the modeling board for the first large definitive coil. Each succeeding coil is welded inside and outside to the coil beneath it. After every three coils, the clay is left to stiffen so the form does not collapse of its own ever-increasing weight during construction. Large and small sculptures are made by building with slabs. They are textured before or after the piece is formed. Corners are either mitered and joined neatly with snug invisible seams; or the slabs may be lapped with edges pressed together so all finger-marked junctures are exposed in a more casual interpretation. In another method, combustible core supports, such as newspaper or excelsior that burn away in the firing, provide an armature for the clay as it is built and while it dries.

A real timesaving technique for forming large sculptures is that of throwing a hollow core on the wheel, then building and modeling on this base. When this method is used, if the throwing process is employed as a means, not a goal, the wheel-thrown sculpture will not become an assemblage of pots and cylinders, but it can be a real work of art. During any of these methods of construction, paddling and hand modeling manipulate the clay. The objective in building a hollow form is to achieve a structure with adequate amounts of clay in the right places, with walls of even thickness, so the clay shell may be manipulated into a form that will dry and fire successfully.

Tools for forming a sculpture are simple and easily obtained. Cutting devices such as a knife and metal loop tools are necessary for hollowing out a solid form, for cutting away excess clay, and for refining surfaces. Cutting tools are

available in sizes for very small forms to special tools for large sculptures. A wooden modeling tool with one end blunted and the other end toothed is useful. Other texturing tools that you can develop for your own ceramic interpretations are a matter of personal style. The most valuable tools are the fingers. They communicate the sculptor's imagery directly as he manipulates the clay.

A coarse open sculpture clay containing 20 to 30 percent fine grog gives a desirable texture. It makes clay more porous, which helps prevent cracks when the clay is dried and fired. As the work is moistened repeatedly during formation, an open porous clay soaks up water. Keep unused clay covered with plastic while you work.

Basic geometric forms are easy to shape. Grapefruit-size lumps of moist clay are beaten and kneaded. Shape them into balls, then wrap them in plastic so they stay moist. Pat or bang each ball until you have some fairly accurate cubes, cylinders, cones, or spheres, but do not strive for mechanical perfection, which could be monotonous. These geometric forms can be textured and altered in endless variations and modifications.

TRIO. *Raul Coronel. Wheel thrown, hand shaped. 6'. Umber to black. Courtesy of the artist.*

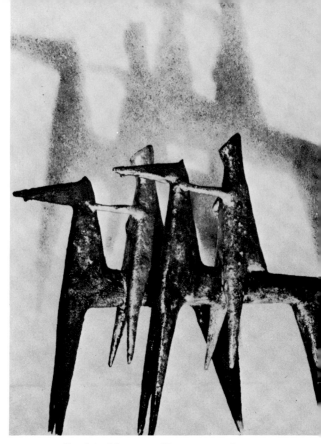

CAVALIERS. *Patriciu Mateescu. Terra cotta. Courtesy of the artist.*

THE FAMILY. *Patriciu Mateescu, Romania. Terra cotta. A harmonious and human grouping of functional forms. Courtesy of the artist.*

ARBRE EN FLEURS. *Patriciu Mateescu. Stoneware. Courtesy of the artist.*

JARDIN ENCANTADO. *Raul Coronel. Wheel-thrown forms combined with slabs.*
5' high. Natural brown stoneware, reduction fired. Courtesy of the artist.

THE CLIFF. *Gail Kristensen. Slab and coil construction. Light buff stoneware with a manganese dioxide wash. 24" high. Courtesy of the artist.*

SCULPTURE FROM GEOMETRIC FORMS

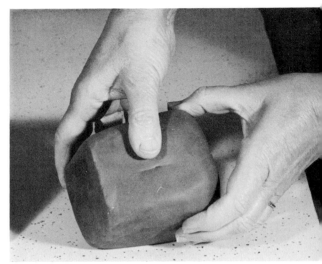

Shape a square form by banging and rolling a clay lump to make rounded edges.

To hollow out a solid cube, cut it apart with a nylon cord, taking care to avoid distorting the two parts.

Carefully scoop out clay with a wire-loop modeling tool. Make the walls of even thickness.

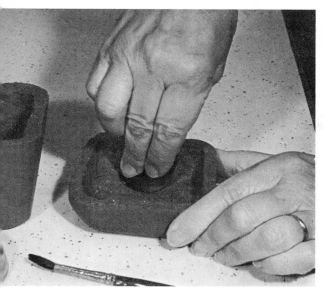

Continue shaping the interior with a rubber kidney. Wet the cut edges carefully without distorting them.

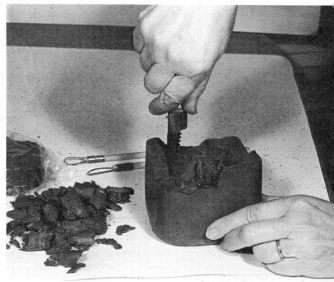

A toothed apple-coring knife is an excellent tool for digging out clay. The pointed end is cut off. Hollow out both sections of the form to make an asymmetrical covered box. By slanting the knife downward when the sections were cut apart, the lid will fit securely. Avoid distorting cut edges.

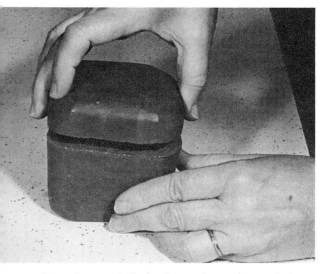

Press the two shells firmly together and smooth the juncture. Forms like this can be textured, carved, or stacked.

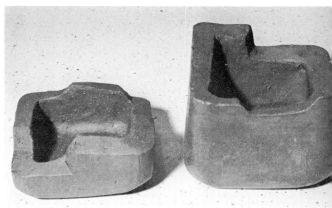

The interior of each part is smoothly finished with a small rubber kidney.

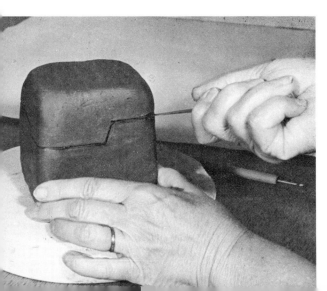

A larger block is carved apart to make a sculptured functional form. Notice that the fettling knife blade slants downward toward the center of the block. Swing the knife around the center of the block as you make straight cuts, but avoid distorting the cut edges.

SCULPTURE FROM
GEOMETRIC FORMS — CUBES

The blocks are textured on all sides except the top and bottom planes.

Form a tall rectangular column. Mark off unequal sections and cut them apart with a nylon cutting cord. Avoid disturbing the top and bottom planes where the blocks were cut apart, or they will not reassemble with ease.

Allow the blocks to become firm, but not leather hard. As each block is positioned, texturing should be a contrast to the texture below it. Here a bottle cap rolls one texture over another kind of texture.

SCULPTURE FROM A CYLINDER

An untextured block can add still more variety. If this project will be fired, all blocks must be hollowed, with openings between sections and at least one opening to the outside to allow moisture to escape.

A large tapered coil is rolled out on the table. Each end is cut flat, with the lower end cut so it slants back when the column is stood on end. The clay is very pliable grogged red sculpture clay. With the left hand bracing the form, the right hand bends it forward.

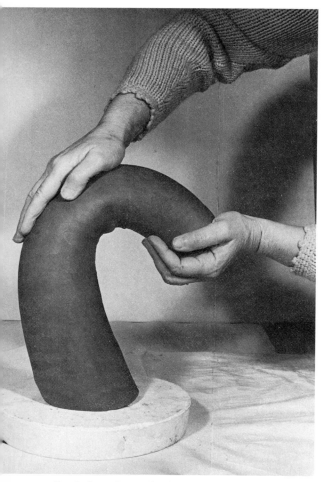

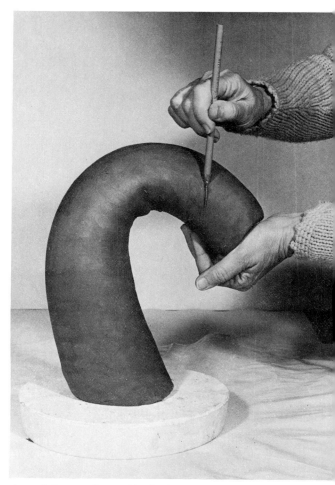

Bend the column slowly with one hand while the other hand braces it.

A mark is scored to guide the limit of the cutting knife.

Slice through the center of the cylinder's top end to split it apart, always bracing with one hand.

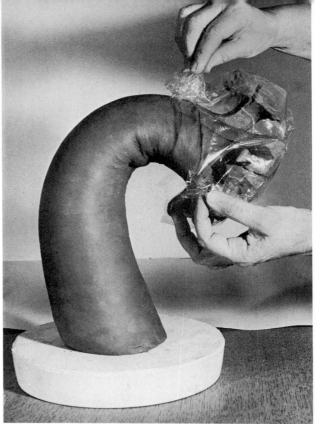

When work is interrupted, even for a short time, it should be protected with a sheet of plastic to prevent it from drying out.

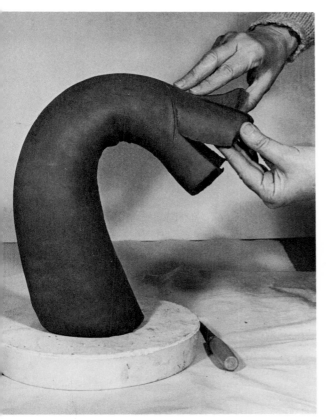

Cut across the first cut to make four quarter sections, using the scored mark as a guide to limit the length of the cuts. Bend each section back.

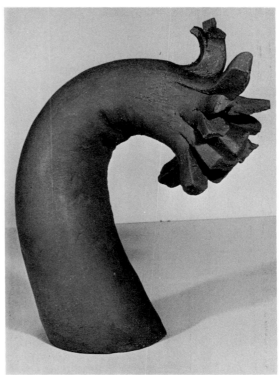

Cut sections are split and resplit. If the form is to be fired, it must be hollowed out from the back.

VESSEL COVERED BY A CRASHED BALL. *Kurt and Gerda Spurey. White porcelain, 7" high. Thrown and molded. Courtesy of the artists.*

Sculpture. Joanna Price. Made from wheel-thrown segments, coiled and combined. Stoneware. Courtesy of the artist.

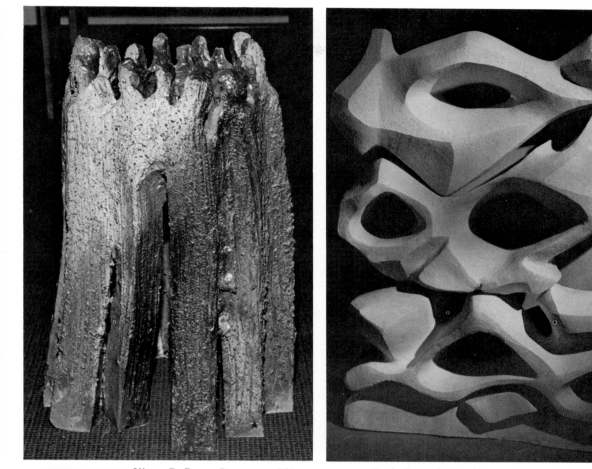

COUNCIL OF MEN. *Victor R. Brosz. Stoneware, 26"
high. Mr. Brosz is Associate Professor of Art,
University of Calgary, Alberta, Canada. Courtesy
of the artist.*

FORMS. *Raul Coronel. Hand-formed stoneware
sculpture. Courtesy of the artist.*

Footed dome. Susanne G. Stephenson. Stoneware. White, black, and orange, with gold luster. Courtesy of the artist.

THE SMUSLAW. *Raymond Grimm. Willamina clay stoneware, reduced. Muted slips. Mounted on brass. Courtesy of the artist.* Photo by Wes Guderian.

HOLLOWED-OUT SCULPTURE*

The design for a hollowed-out animal sculpture may stylize or even exaggerate the animal's distinguishing features. Each species has identifying traits by which it is recognized. Very few animals stand firmly erect on all four feet with head facing front. Their typical gestures reveal the instinctive manner of their behavior in their natural habitat under varying circumstances.

Before an animal project is begun, it is rewarding to do some research on the animal. For example, we discover that bears have poor eyesight and carry their heads in a low-slung peering manner while they amble along seeking bits of roots, berries, and small insects. Members of the cat family slink along with a graceful movement. The hippopotamus loves to relax in sluggish rivers where he lies partly submerged with his head resting on the riverbank or upon a fellow creature. Although he seems to be half asleep, his small ears are alert for alien or menacing sounds.

The most prominent part of a hippopotamus is his huge ugly head. With an impressive body weight of 5,000 to 8,000 pounds, his head alone may weigh 1,000 pounds! This massive head has bulbous, protruding, thick-lidded eyes that open at the side rather than in front. Heavy jowls and a square bulky jaw are other distinguishing features that the sculptor can accentuate or exaggerate logically. The bony structure of an animal's head has well-defined planes and ridges that should be emphasized. Parts of the body that protrude, such as ears, tail, legs, and feet, require special study to determine whether they should be supported by being curved against the body. These projections will need care, too, when the sculpture is dried.

A sculpture should dry slowly so it does not crack. If a crack does appear, some clay of the same consistency is worked into it, then the area is sprayed lightly with water. A damp cloth

draped loosely over finished sculpture will promote even drying. It can be removed from time to time, then replaced. It may be sprayed occasionally if the piece seems to dry too rapidly. Too fast drying of narrow projections such as ears can cause them to crack loose from the larger form.

The illustrated project is a small sculpture of a baby hippo as it appears when partly submerged. A baby hippo's head is unusually large in proportion to its body size. Its hide is rough and thick. An appropriate clay for this form is soft red sculpture clay with 10 to 20 percent grog, purchased moist from the supplier. It fires at cone 06–04. A solid cylinder is formed and slapped down to flatten the base. The clay is pressed into rough form with a short length of a two-by-four. Clay must be compacted by pounding or rolling before it is shaped. If a clay form is carved from a block of clay that is not compacted, it will shrink unevenly when it is dried and fired, resulting in a lumpy surface. Fingers and modeling tools, manipulated in any desired manner, develop the general shape. Clay is added bit by bit or cut away wherever necessary.

When the final form is attained, and the clay has become firm but not leather hard, the sculpture is turned over and cushioned on four soft lumps of clay. These lumps must be *softer* than the clay of the sculptured piece or they will press dents into it. Hollow out the form with a metal loop tool until all walls are about ½ inch thick. Walls over an inch thick are likely to crack during the firing process.

The hippo's features are given a final modeling with a moist sponge, and small thick ears are added. The spots where the ears will be joined to the head are scored and painted with slip for better adhesion. When the sculpture has become leather hard, it is textured with a metal brush tapped lightly over it. The piece is left to dry slowly. Small projections are wrapped or covered loosely with a damp cloth that can be

* From an article by the author, which appeared in *Ceramics Monthly.*

sprayed with water occasionally to slow down the drying process and avoid the hazards of cracks. It is best to avoid making long or thin projections.

Firing ceramic sculpture is a critical procedure because these clay forms usually have thicker walls with more variations than most pottery forms. The hippo is set on several pieces of insulation brick to raise it from the kiln floor so atmospheric moisture can escape from the interior of the form. Although pieces may be bone dry before the kiln is started, they are given a heat-soaking for two or more hours with the kiln turned very low and the door partly open. Large kilns fully stacked with sculpture must have several hours of preliminary heating. Even bone-dry pieces contain atmospheric and chemical moisture that must be driven off slowly. It must work its way out of the thick clay between minute clay particles. Kiln heat must be raised with extreme slowness. Many kiln loads of ceramic sculpture have been ruined by too rapid preliminary heating. When the kiln has cooled and the door is opened, broken bits and pieces bring dismay and disappointment over lost hours of careful work.

A heat rise of 25° F. to 50° F. per hour for the first few hours is not too slow. It is advisable to leave the peephole open at least through 1300° F. or until all moisture is dissipated. Test it by holding a piece of cool glass close to the peephole. If no moisture appears on the glass, you may assume the ware is dry. If you are having ceramic sculpture custom fired, it is important that the kiln operator understands the peculiar requirements of firing sculpture.

When the demonstration piece has been bisque fired and is completely cool, it is ready for glazing. Immerse it in water, then withdraw it quickly. Two immersions should be adequate for red sculpture clay, at least one for stoneware. Excess water is emptied at once. Just sponging off a piece is not usually sufficient; thorough wetting of the bisque allows glaze to go on smoothly instead of collecting in uneven lumps. Some of the glaze soaks in for better bonding with the clay.

The baby hippo is given three medium coats of glaze. The first coat is brushed on smoothly with a soft wide brush. Before the glaze dries, it is gently rubbed in with a finger to work it into pores and crevices. Second and third coats are brushed crosswise to each preceding coat. Some sculptors prefer to glaze their work very lightly for accents and highlights so the rough clay is very much in evidence, while others do not glaze at all. It is entirely a matter of personal preference.

The demonstration sculpture is left in a warm place to dry completely. Because of the thorough wetting, it will take extra time to dry. Although glazed bisque can be fired a little faster than raw ware, slow firing is always worth the time it takes. If any pinholes have appeared when the glaze has dried, a *clean* dry finger can be rubbed lightly back and forth across the pinholes to work some of the dry glaze into them. When completed and fired, the hippo sculpture may be cemented to a ceramic base which follows the contours of the sculpture.

A HOLLOWED-OUT ANIMAL SCULPTURE

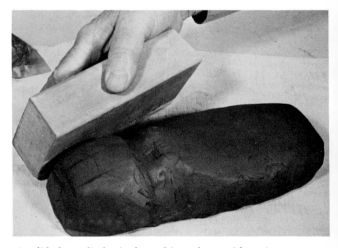

A solid clay cylinder is slapped into shape with a piece of two-by-four. Compacting the clay will prevent uneven shrinkage when it is fired.

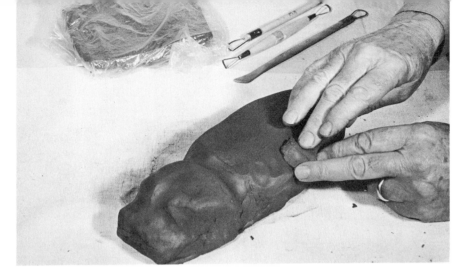

Soft clay is added to build out the form; apply small pieces and press them firmly into place. Keep the moist clay supply covered with plastic to prevent it from drying.

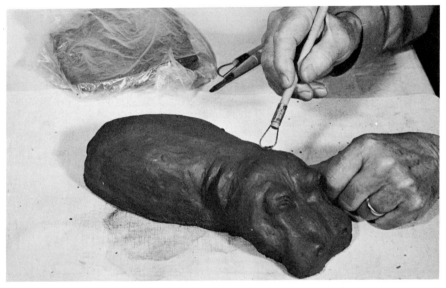

A loop modeling tool cuts away excess clay; fingers and modeling tools shape the essential features and bony structure.

The form is hollowed out from the bottom.

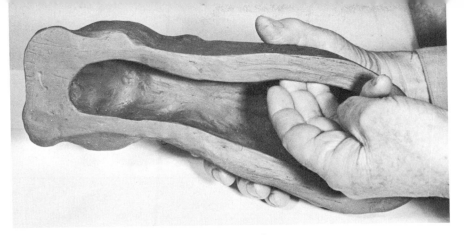

All sides are left approximately ½ inch thick or less.

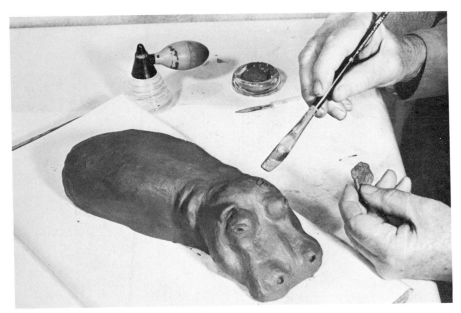

*Small ears and the areas where they will be attached are scored
and slip-painted before the ears are applied. Clay for the ears must
be kneaded and compacted, so it will not shrink excessively
and crack loose from the body when it is dried and fired.*

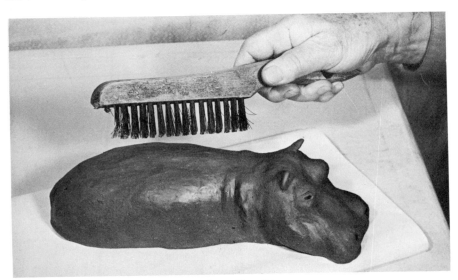

*When the leather-hard body is textured, avoid striking
the ears and cracking them loose.*

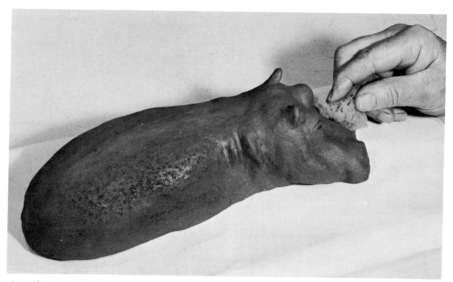

A moist sponge gives final modeling refinements and brings grog to the surface for a rough texture.

Baby Hippo. Certain features are emphasized to show the animal's relaxed watchfulness. (For the description of glazing this form, see the section on glazes.)

HORNED ANIMAL. *Charles Lakofsky. Courtesy of the Butler Institute of American Art.*

BRAHMA BULL. *Paul Bogatay. Courtesy of the Butler Institute of American Art.*

ARSHYLE ELEPHANT. *Donald P. Taylor. Stoneware, cone 10. Bernard slip and light application of low-fire glazes. 11" long, 7½" wide, 8" high.* Photos by Donald P. Taylor.

BOUC *(male goat). Patriciu Mateescu. Courtesy of the artist.*

Hanging sculptural units. Raul Coronel. Stoneware, wheel thrown, flattened, reshaped, textured, and cut. Polychromatic color. From a group made for and installed in the Landmark Hotel, Las Vegas, Nevada. Sizes range from 1' to 7'.

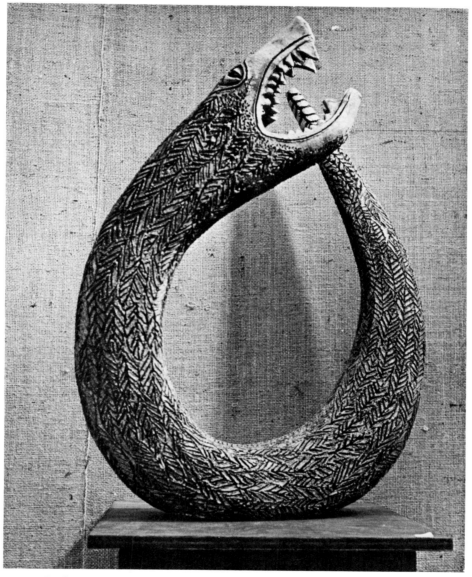

VIBORA. *Raul Coronel. Stoneware, wheel thrown and hand shaped. 24" high. Brown with black lines. Courtesy of the artist.*

SCULPTURE FROM CLAY SLABS

A slab-built paper core sculpture is demonstrated by sculptor Ruth Tepping. Because she works with soft clay, she starts with a dowel stick armature wound with crushed newspaper to provide bulk and strength. The dowel stick armature is anchored in a heavy wooden disk supported on a stemless bench wheel. A straight stick armature that can be pulled out easily is the only practical one for a clay sculpture that will be fired. While the newspaper core is being constructed, Ruth temporarily holds it together with ordinary string until she has applied the first slab. The paper is shrinkable and expendable. Because it will absorb moisture from the clay, it can be removed easily by being pulled out at the bottom. Or it can be left inside the clay where it will burn out later in the kiln.

When the paper-covered armature is ready, Ruth starts to build with large ½-inch- to ¾-inch-thick slabs cut from a 25-pound block of wedged grogged sculpture clay. The first thick slabs make a sturdy base. Changing to thinner slabs as she builds upward, she constructs a strong clay shell to work on. Although the clay is moist, it is sustained by plenty of grog.

Ruth begins her work from a standing position, vigorously pushing, squeezing, and forcing the thick clay into place with the heel of her hand. She keeps the clay moist by wetting her fingers in a bowl of water nearby. When clay completely covers the paper core, it is paddled into shape. From here on, it is mostly a matter of applying wads of clay from which to model the features. A perpendicular line is scored down the center of the face to divide it into two planes. Eye sockets are cut deep. The mouth is not a slot cut in the face but is a full protruding form; clay is applied for modeling the lips and nose. Clay is applied in layers for the hair mass. All additions of clay are pressed firmly with the heel of the hand. Ruth works all over the form,

refining and modeling the hair and features, at the same time texturing the surface with a wire-loop texturing tool. As soon as the clay can hold its form well, the sculpture is lifted off its dowel stick. The paper core has become moist and is easily pulled out. The form dries for two or more weeks before it is fired.

When Ruth Tepping fires her sculptures, she begins with an overnight heat-soaking period with heat turned to low, the top-loading kiln lid propped open a crack, and peepholes left open. The next day she turns the kiln to medium heat where it stays until the temperature reaches 1000° F. Then she turns it to high. Because her kiln is small, this is not too fast to fire her work. Large kilns fully loaded with sculpture take considerably longer.

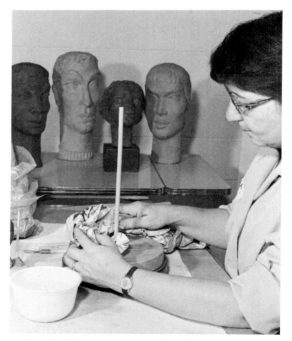

A dowel stick armature is anchored in a hole drilled in the center of a heavy wooden disk, supported on a stemless bench wheel. Ruth Tepping wraps twisted newspaper around the armature to begin building a core that will support the slab shell of a portrait sculpture.

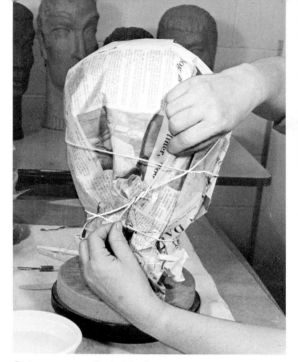

String temporarily holds the paper core together until the first slabs are placed.

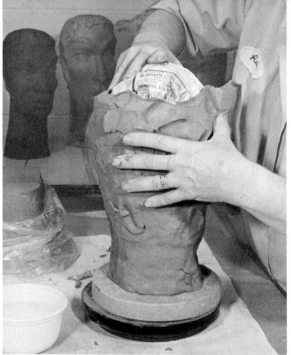

Changing to thinner slabs as she builds upward, Ruth constructs a strong shell to work on. She vigorously squeezes, pushes, and forces the thick clay into place with the heel of her hand.

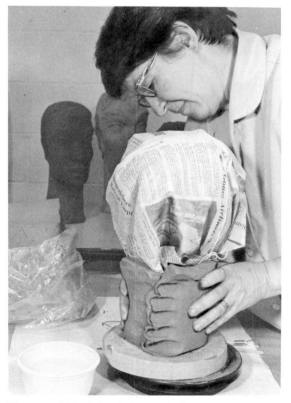

The very thick slabs of the sturdy base are pressed firmly together.

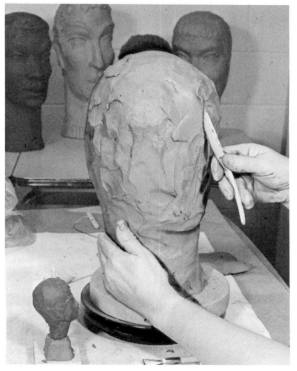

A perpendicular line is scored down the center of the face to separate it into two planes. From here on, it becomes a matter of modeling with added clay. Clay additions will be applied for nose, mouth, and hair. She works now from a small clay sketch previously modeled.

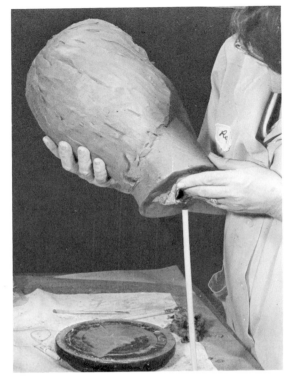

The clay is left to dry a little from time to time; when it can hold its form well, it is lifted off the armature. Much of the moist paper core is pulled out. The dowel stick is pulled from its wooden base before the form is returned to the bench wheel.

Some of the neck clay is cut away as Ruth gives it a forward slant. She explains that the mouth is a full protruding form and not a slot in the face. Clay is applied to the mouth so she can model the lips.

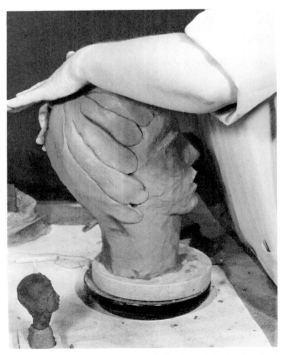

Additions of clay are pressed firmly with the heel of the hand. Clay is applied for modeling the lips and nose. Long flat layers are applied for the hair mass.

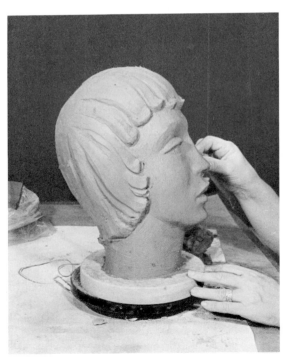

Final modeling is done with a texturing tool, as she works all over the form, refining and modeling hair and features.

The completed form.

Stoneware sculptures. Ruth Tepping. Mrs. Tepping constructs one of her portrait sculptures in one lecture period.

Small sculputure. Ruth Tepping. Photographs of Mrs. Tepping's sculptures by Polly Rothenberg.

WOMAN WITH A SCARF. *Ruth Tepping.*

WOMEN GOING FOR WATER. *Ruth Tepping. The body form of these miniature sculptures is made of a truncated triangular slab that is textured with clay texture stamps and texture wheels. The slab is rolled into a cone shape. The heads are small clay balls with tiny expressive features modeled. Arms are small coils.*

MOTHER AND CHILD. *Ruth Tepping.*

CLAY COIL SCULPTURE

A small clay "sketch" of a larger planned form is very helpful in guiding the construction of a coil sculpture. Adjustable calipers are used to check measurements of the clay sketch against measurements of the emerging sculpture to keep it in proper proportion.

Before work is begun, lay a sheet of heavy plastic over a modeling board. Tuck the sides of the plastic sheet under the board. When work is interrupted, the sheeting can be brought up and over it to keep the clay moist. Draw the outline of the planned sculpture's base directly on the plastic sheet. The first thick coil is pressed firmly against the plastic on this marked outline. Coils for sculpture are thick and flat. The clay from which they are cut must be well wedged and compacted so the sculpture dries evenly and without sagging. First coils are heavy; successive coils can be thinner as they near the top of the form. After each coil addition, the clay is thumbed down, inside and outside the wall, to weld it to the coil beneath it. After every three rows, the clay must be allowed to firm up or "set" so the soft clay does not collapse from its ever-increasing weight during construction. After a few coils have been laid, slab cross walls are constructed to strengthen and brace the walls.

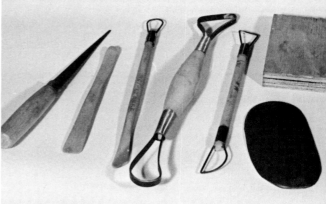

Tools used for this sculpture are simple and basic.

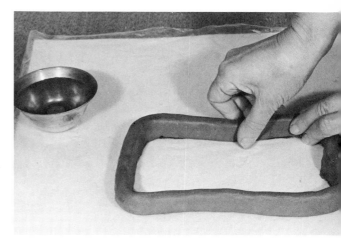

The first thick coil is pressed snugly against the modeling board.

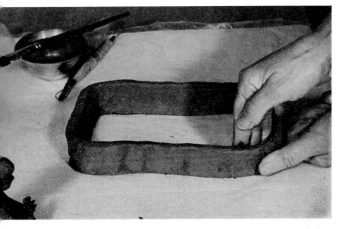

Second and third coils are added and thumb-welded down, inside and outside.

The form is essentially two rectangular blocks and a sphere. More clay is added and thumbed down.

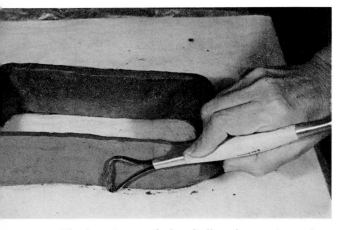

The form is smoothed and allowed to set for a short time.

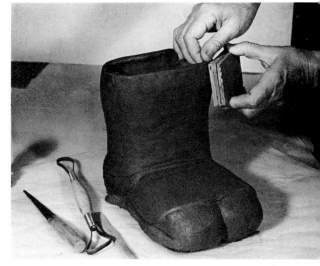

A section of board paddled all over the form knits and pulls it together. Construction is guided by a clay sketch.

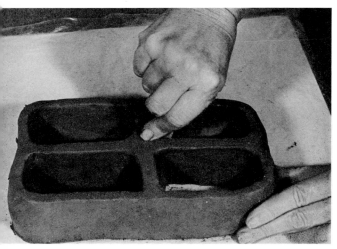

Crosspieces are fastened firmly to the inside of the base to strengthen and brace walls from sagging outward.

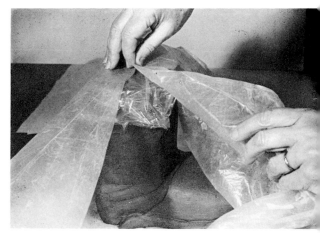

Whenever the work is interrupted, plastic sheeting is brought up from beneath the board and fastened over the work. It must be kept in moist condition.

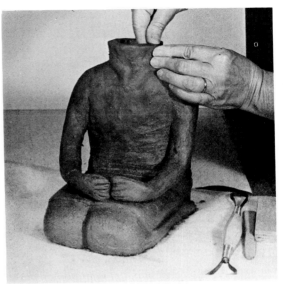

The arms are made hollow by forming them over a long twist of newspaper. It will burn out in the firing. The top end of an arm coil is smacked firmly into position, one hand braces the clay from the inside.

A flattened coil provides clay for the neck. The sculpture is formed freely without striving for exactness of detail, just suggestions of form.

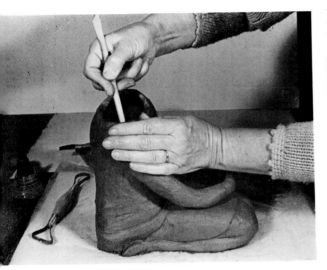

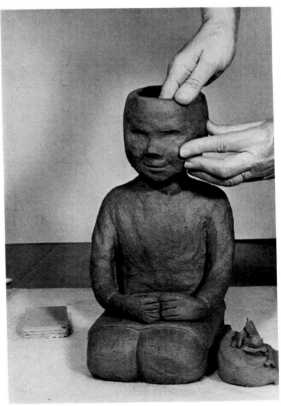

A modeling tool with a wire loop end cuts clay away from inside the top end of the arm to expose the twist of newspaper core. Air must be allowed to assist in combustion when the paper is exposed to kiln heat.

Coiling the head is similar to coiling a bowl. It forms a clay shell from which features can be modeled. Some head detail must be shaped before the top is closed in; eye sockets are pressed in and clay is added for nose, cheeks, and lips. The head shell includes most of the hair mass cavity.

Fingers are indicated and flowers are part of the main mass; sculpture clay does not lend itself well to fussy details. The hair is modeled partly from thin added clay, partly from the head shell. Children's heads are large in proportion to their bodies. The brown clay is not glazed.

Ceramic tomb figure. Chinese, Tang dynasty (A.D. 616–906). The lady taking a stately step depicts a person of unquestioned high position. Courtesy of the Metropolitan Museum of Art, New York, Rogers Fund.

DIOGENES. *Lois Maher. Unglazed red clay. 2½' high. Courtesy of the American Art Clay Company.*

FEMALE BUST. *Raul Coronel. Black wheel-thrown stoneware, hand shaped. 22" high. Courtesy of the artist.*

GIRL WITH A BRAID. *Helen Barlow. Bronzed stoneware. Courtesy of the artist.*

BIRD MAN. *Raul Coronel. Wheel-thrown stoneware, hand shaped. 4'. Natural stoneware with black in the lines. Courtesy of the artist.*

WOMAN AND CHILD. *Raul Coronel. Wheel-thrown stoneware, hand shaped. 42" high. Natural (reduced) stoneware with black in the lines. Courtesy of the artist.*

Four women. Edwin Scheier. Wheel thrown, hand shaped. Courtesy of the artist.

THE FAMILY. *Vivienne Eisner. A study in planes. Courtesy of the Tepping Studio Supply Company.*

Sculpture. Elly Kuch. West Germany. Gray stoneware with white glaze.
Courtesy of the artist. **Photo by Kuch.**

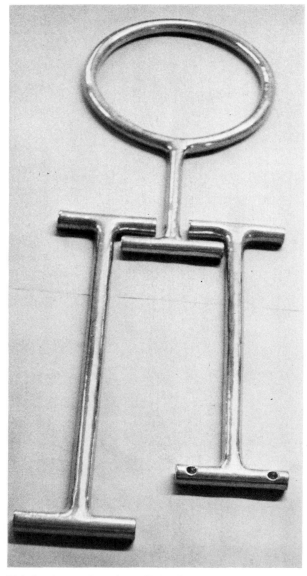

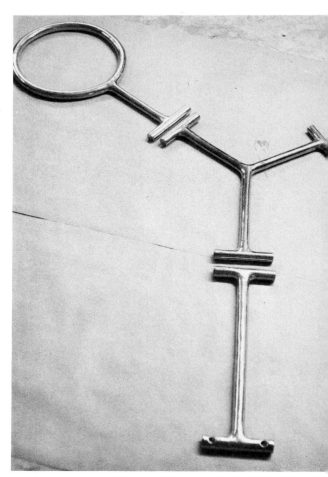

Tubular forms. Patrick McCormick. Stoneware, 1" in diameter. Horizontal compositions that have flexibility in placement, 50" long. Silver luster. Courtesy of the artist.

Tubular forms. Patrick McCormick. Earthenware with silver luster, 50" long. A linear development of segmented lines and proximity placement. Courtesy of the artist.

Tubular construction. Patrick McCormick. Unglazed stoneware, 36" long.
Mr. McCormick teaches at Western Washington State University at Bellingham.
Courtesy of the artist.

Anna Malicka Zamorska in her shop in Warsaw,
Poland. Courtesy of the artist. Photo by Tadeusz
Szwed.

BUBBLE-ROEBUCK. *Anna Malicka Zamorska. Themes are traditional; handling of the clay is modern. Courtesy of the artist.*

PRINCESS. *Anna Malicka Zamorska. Courtesy of the artist.*

ZODIAC FIGURES: MERMAID AND NEPTUNE. *Anna Malicka Zamorska. Courtesy of the artist.*

TWIN BUBBLE. *Anna Malicka Zamorska. Courtesy of the artist.*

Ceramic fountain. Raul Coronel. Separate parts of the fountain are wheel thrown and altered; after they are fired, they are assembled on location. Umber-colored stoneware, 12 feet tall. The fountain's organic design is especially suited to the exotic vegetation surrounding it. Designed for and installed in the home of Isadore Familian, Beverly Hills, California. Courtesy of the artist.

ARCHITECTURAL CERAMICS

Murals

Dramatic interior wall compositions enrich the durable planes and volumes of today's architecture. Concrete and curtain wall construction, exposed architectural framework, and glass walls that bring the out-of-doors indoors generate a desire for an appropriate environment that fulfills our emotional and practical needs. In a room where a glass wall discloses a real mountain, lake, or city skyline, clearly the requirement is for interior wall compositions that have some strength of their own. The startling clarity of fused glass, the pattern and color of cascading fabric, or the chunkiness of a bold ceramic relief can aesthetically extend abstract forms of architecture and enhance plain walls with form, texture, and color.*

Muralists today are not content with confining their attention to their commissioned wall. They are cognizant of the emotional and psychological impact of the immediate surroundings. Indeed, they strive to integrate the mural design into the total environment so the viewer is wrapped in the pleasurable role of becoming a participant and not simply a viewer. At the present time, architects are just beginning to invite the muralist or sculptor to become a member of the designing team during the all-important preliminary planning stages. But as the artist grows and educates himself in the needs and functions of the architect, and as enlightened clients generate a demand, the true architectural wall may become a more familiar part of building design.

In the strict meaning of the word, any tile (or tiles) with a design on it, or tiles that are individually segments of a larger design, and

---

* From an article by the author, which appeared in *Design* magazine.

that are cemented to a wall, may be called a mural. The word "mural" is of French origin and means "on or of a wall." Ceramic murals in any size may be designed with geometric tiles (or slabs) or with free-form segments assembled as a mosaic. Thus large murals can be constructed even by the craftsman whose kiln space limits the size of pieces he may fire. If free-form pieces are to be assembled, a scale drawing or plan is prepared so that junctures form logical lines in the design. When the mural is a large one, it is helpful to make a small model so that design problems are solved before actual construction begins.

MEDICINE AROUND THE WORLD. *Raul Coronel. This tremendous mural is 1,000 square feet. Asymmetrical segments are intricately shaped as an important part of the design. They vary in relief thickness from one inch to four inches. Hand-sculptured stoneware in polychromatic color. Designed for and installed in Miles Laboratory, Elkhart, Indiana. Courtesy of the artist.* Photo by Alex A. Tschumakow.

Detail of "Medicine Around the World."

Eminent sculptor, Raul Coronel, of California, carves one of his enormous architectural lamps. Courtesy of the artist.

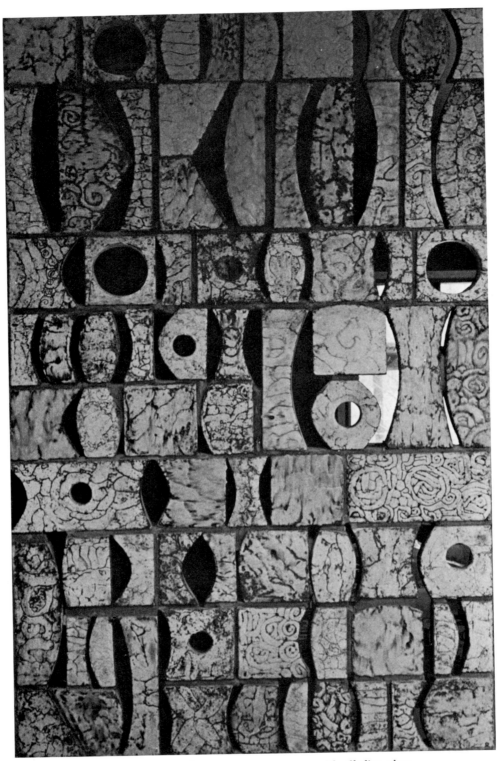

Ceramic wall. Nicholas Vergette. Coarse groggy stoneware with alkaline glaze over copper oxide rubbed into the body. Designed for and installed in the home of Dr. I. Kua Chou, Murphysboro, Illinois. Courtesy of the artist.

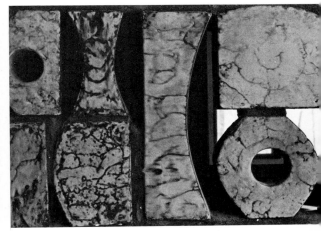

Detail of the wall with the distinctive coil segments Mr. Vergette uses in many of his compositions.

The wall silhouetted from inside the study.

*Nicholas Vergette brushes glaze on one unit of a twelve-unit project he
created for Southern Illinois University campus at Carbondale. Segments of
each section were made by compressing coiled clay into wooden forms. The
sections were fired, glazed, and assembled. On the worktable are models
of the units, ranging from 6 to 14 feet high. Mr. Vergette teaches at Southern
Illinois University. Courtesy of the artist.*

FRAGMENTS. *Raymond Grimm. Willamina clay mounted on brass. Various muted slips have been applied and burned in with a torch. 3' x 1½'. Courtesy of the artist.*

Mural. Gail Kristensen. Black stoneware with manganese dioxide. Courtesy of the artist.

Raku wall. Paul Rayar, the Netherlands. Two hundred sixty hand-formed smoked raku tiles, reduced in sawdust, in brilliant reds, blues, and greens. Designed for and installed in the City Hall building in Dordrecht, the Netherlands. Courtesy of the artist. Photo by Cees Mookhoek.

Raku Wall by Paul Rayar

Paul Rayar, architectural artist of Epen, the Netherlands, has adapted the technique of raku for work in architectural murals. Paul, who began as a painter, discovered in the mural a potential for expression not found within the confines of the canvas. The wall, he believes, should not be a ground for decoration, but should itself be the mural. The wall illustrated is the first raku wall in Europe. It is installed in the City Hall building in Dordrecht, the Netherlands.

The 260 hand-formed raku smoked tiles, taken red hot from the kiln and reduced in sawdust, give a rare texture in sparkling red, blue, and green colors in a silver speckled metallic gloss. Because the eye is not engaged in interpreting the various forms, colors, and spaces, the viewer neither accepts nor rejects what he sees; he only marvels at what he feels. The viewer himself becomes an organic part of the environment, no longer merely an onlooker.

To install his raku slabs, Paul Rayar uses a water soluble glue that dries quickly. Each newly affixed tile is separated from the tile below by pegs to hold it in place for the few moments until the glue sets. The spaces between the tiles are filled with regular grout made of sand, cement, and color. For a stoneware ceramic wall installed on the exterior of the University of Amsterdam, Mr. Rayar uses a two-component epoxy made especially for heavy exterior work.

Paul Rayar (left) *and Jacques Bouman* (right) *install individual raku tiles. A sketch of the design, marked on the wall, guides placement of each tile. Notice small pegs between tiles at the top, which hold tiles apart for the few moments until the tile glue sets. Courtesy of the artist.* Photo by Cees Mookhoek.

General close-up view of the raku wall.

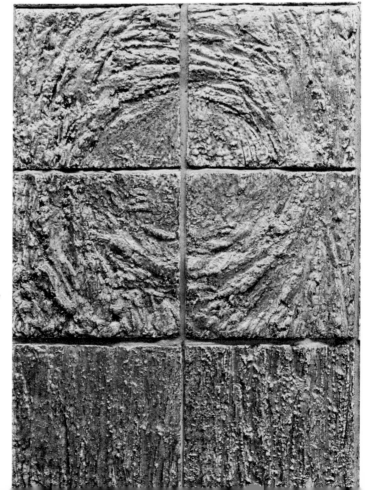

Detail of tiles of Paul Rayar's wall.
Each tile is hand formed. Notice the heavy
grogged character of the raku clay body.
Courtesy of the artist.
Photos by Cees Mookhoek.

SECTION 5

OTHER
CERAMIC FORMS

RAKU

The raku ware developed by early Oriental craftsmen as small ceremonial teabowls was distinguished by its hand-formed character and its organic textured surface. Although the materials and the firing methods are essentially unchanged today, craftsmen are reducing the glaze fire in a variety of ways to achieve some wonderful surface effects. The informal simplicity of raku is especially appealing to young craftsmen of our time. They are making objects as tall as twenty inches, pieces with handles and lids, sculptural forms, and murals, using the same basic methods.

A bisqued clay form is covered with a glaze that fuses from approximately 1600°F. to 1800°F. When the glaze is thoroughly dry, the object is put into a hot kiln by means of long raku tongs. Asbestos gloves should be worn when these tongs are used. The glaze firing is observed from time to time until it starts to melt and turns shiny. The piece is pulled from the hot kiln with the tongs. As soon as its bright orange heat turns to dull red (in a matter of seconds), it is thrust into a container of combustibles such as sawdust, pine needles, or dried leaves, and is covered with more of the same material. The lid is clamped on quickly to shut off oxygen in the air and make a reduction atmosphere. After a wait of about three minutes, the piece is removed from the container with the tongs and quenched in a bucket of water to "hold" the effects of reduction. The piece can be air cooled instead of being quenched in water, but some of the effects may oxidize away.

A clay body for raku ware must be porous enough to withstand the dual thermal shocks it encounters when it is thrust into the hot kiln for glaze firing instead of warming up slowly in a cold kiln, and when it is plunged into water for cooling. A heavily grogged stoneware clay (about 40 percent grog) should work well although the bisque fire is brought to only cone 04. If the bisque is fired higher and the ware becomes dense, it is likely to crack when it is put into the hot kiln for glaze firing or when it is quenched in water. Many factors influence the results of this exotic process. To avoid unpleasant roughness in the glaze, be sure to allow the bright orange heat to change to dull red so the molten glaze congeals before you thrust it into the metal container or bricked-in area (if done outdoors) containing combustibles. If pieces are reduced longer than three minutes, the glaze may become dark, smoky, and blackened. When the glaze contains such chemicals as metal oxides or carbonates, iridescent metallic lusters may appear on the fired surface of the wire. The chance "happening," partly controlled by the choice of glaze, the timing, surface manipulation, and the character of the reducing combustibles, accounts for much of the continuing charm of raku.

The clay body used in the demonstration project is a ready prepared moist stoneware

sculpture clay with additional grog added at the wedging stage. When it has been thoroughly blended, the clay is shaped into a hand-formed bowl with walls that are not too thin. Some additional grog is pressed into the surface of the finished shape for texture. White slip (engobe) is painted over the upper two-thirds of the small bowl. Thrown forms, finger-shaped bowls, or slab shapes with firmly welded junctures can make handsome raku projects. Coiled forms are likely to crack where the coils are joined, unless a really superb job of blending the coils together is accomplished. Although there are usually three prongs on the ends of the tongs where they grasp the clay object, only one prong on each side is likely to take hold of the piece if the walls are not perpendicular. It is sometimes a problem to get a firm grasp on the red hot object unless it is formed with indentations or textured areas on its surface. It is advisable to make a "practice run" through the required manipulations of using the tongs, handling the sawdust container lid, and plunging the piece into the tub of water, before the actual raku process really begins.

The completed demonstration project is dried and bisque fired to cone 04, which leaves stoneware essentially porous. A low-firing transparent glaze, poured into the cooled piece, is rolled around and poured out again. The upper two-thirds of the exterior is brushed with glaze over the white slip, leaving the lower third unglazed. The glaze used for this project fuses between 1600°F. and 1800°F. It is as follows:

20% Potash Feldspar
80% Gerstley Borate

A small amount of binder helps the glaze stick to the bisque when the object is grasped with raku tongs. Regular glaze gum (methyl cellulose) is a satisfactory binder. The addition of 3 percent copper carbonate added to the dry ingredients of the glaze produces some exciting color effects when the piece is reduced in the smoking process. All the dry ingredients are combined with enough water to make a medium thin glaze; they are mixed in a kitchen blender turned to low speed.

When the glaze is completely dry, the bowl is grasped firmly with raku tongs and is set carefully and quickly into the center of a small hot front-loading kiln; the door is closed immediately to avoid loss of heat. If the temperature in the kiln is near 1700°F., it should not take long for the glaze to melt. When the glaze turns shiny, the hot glowing piece is grasped with the tongs, removed from the kiln, and carefully lowered into the container of dried combustibles. The container for this project is a three-gallon metal bucket half filled with sand and a top layer of two or three inches of sawdust. There is a minor combustion flame-up as the hot bowl ignites the sawdust. Just before the metal cover is clamped down on the metal bucket, a pan of additional sawdust is emptied on top of the smoldering form. The lid is important because without a cover over the smoking object there is no reducing action. It is essential that room ventilation be adequate and the floor is of concrete if unpleasant hazards are to be avoided when the red hot object is removed from the glaze fire and reduced in burning sawdust indoors.

After three minutes reduction, the lid is removed from the sawdust container. The hot ware is picked up again with raku tongs and lowered into a tub of water. Because the bowl is covered with burned sawdust and smoke, it looks discouragingly messy and is scarcely recognizable. This dirt is all scrubbed away with cleanser as soon as the piece is cool enough to handle.

Robert Piepenburg removes a tall raku bottle from a top-loading kiln.
Courtesy of the artist. Photo by Neil Atkins.

Robert Piepenburg loads glazed raku ware into a "cold" corbel-arched drawer kiln. After the first firing, pottery is loaded into the heated kiln with metal tongs. Courtesy of the artist. Photo by Neil Atkins.

Metal tongs, 36" long, used for removing hot raku ware from hot kilns. The special tongs are designed and made by Robert Piepenburg for use in handling very large raku forms. Courtesy of the artist.

Raku weed vase. Robert Piepenburg. Approximately 16" high. Mr. Piepenburg is the author of Raku Pottery, The Macmillan Co., 1972.

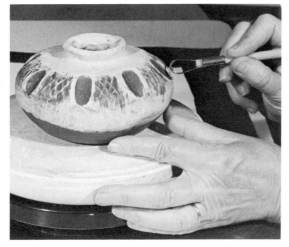

A pinched form is made from grogged stoneware sculpture clay. It is carved and painted with white slip. The lower fourth is left unpainted. When the ware is dry, it is bisque fired to cone 04.

With the tongs, immediately lower the red hot ware into a bucket of sawdust for reduction. As the hot piece approaches the sawdust, it ignites with a minor combustion flame-up.

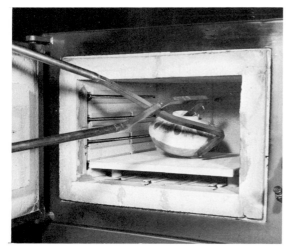

As soon as the glaze melts, the form is removed from the hot kiln with raku tongs.

When additional sawdust has been tossed on top of the smoldering form, a metal lid is clamped on loosely.

After about three minutes reduction, the hot smoky ware is lowered carefully into a bucket of water. When it is cool, it is removed from the bucket and scrubbed with cleanser to remove sawdust and other soil.

Decorative lines can be cut through unfired glaze to expose bare clay that will become black. The dark gray areas to the left and right are luster.

Top view of the fired bowl.

Raku bowl. Don Schaumburg. White with red luster and copper oxide on black body. Mr. Schaumburg teaches at Arizona State University at Tempe. Courtesy of the artist. Photo by Lud Keaton.

Raku vases. Robert Piepenburg. White vase, 22″ high; black vase, 24″ high. From the collection of Joanna and Wilber Price.

Raku form. Peggy Wickham. White with copper accents on green. Wheel thrown, with appliqué design. Buff clay body, grogged with vermiculite. 7″ high. Courtesy of the artist.

Raku vessel with handles. Robert Piepenburg. 7" high. Courtesy of the artist.

CLOUDS OVER MY ORANGE GROVE. *Randall Schmidt.*
Raku cookie jar, 13" high. Courtesy of the artist.

Detail of gray-beard design. Lucien den Arend.

Bearded face form. Lucien den Arend, Holland.
Raku-fired, grogged earthenware clay. The glazed top
is yellow with gold luster. A stamped design was
impressed with a fragment of old gray-beard jug.
15" high. Courtesy of the artist.

Raku forms. Lucien den Arend. Left: red clay body, blackened by reduction.
Top section is a semitransparent white glaze with cobalt oxide decoration.
Right: alkaline glaze over white engobe (slip) with cobalt oxide bands. The
crackle is formed by waiting until the cracking is heard when the piece is pulled
from the glaze fire, then reducing it in sawdust. Courtesy of the artist.

Detail of the small form (left). *Lucien den Arend.*

Raku form. Lucien den Arend. Earthenware clay with grog. The top half is unglazed black (reduced). Interior and lower half are a soft green and luster from reduced copper carbonate. Courtesy of the artist.

Raku slab vase. Lucien den Arend. Earthenware clay with grog. The marks are left from joining with a "bug sticker." Alkaline glaze with cobalt oxide design. The black and dark lustrous areas are results of reduction (smoking). White areas are engobe. 15" high. Courtesy of the artist.

Raku bowl. Lucien den Arend. Paddled earthenware. Low-fire glaze, iron and carborundum, ocher and green. 3½" x 4". Courtesy of the artist.

Raku slab form. Lucien den Arend. Slab built, with grogged earthenware body. Low-fire glaze, green and luster from copper carbonate. 4½" high. Courtesy of the artist.

Raku form. Lucien den Arend. Low-fire glaze with zircon, to make blue black luster. Courtesy of the artist. Lucien den Arend is a talented architectural sculptor in Holland who also likes to work with raku forms.

FUNCTIONAL FORMS

When a ceramic object is meant to be used, it should function efficiently. Not only should it be utilitarian, but it ought to be a joy to use. There is no joy in trying to hold a large mug whose handle is so small only two fingers can squeeze comfortably through it; nor is there pleasure in pouring from a teapot whose lid topples into our cup along with the tea. A pitcher with a really generous handle provides ample leverage for pouring liquids. So sought for is the kind of imaginative hand-formed functional ceramic ware that people really like to use that today an increasing number of craftsmen are devoting at least a portion of their time to this lucrative work. They are proving, too, that functional ceramics can have charm and beauty as well as sturdiness.

Covered jar. Raymond Grimm. Reduction-fired stoneware. This handsome functional form has a forged metal handle. The glaze is green iron, reduction fired, over exposed dark gray body. Courtesy of the artist.

Fifteenth-century Spanish pitcher. This enormous earthenware form, holding nearly eight quarts, is decorated with tin faïence enameled designs; the spout and entire handle are glazed with copper luster. 18½″ high. Pitchers like this were used for dispensing wine and water. Courtesy of the Metropolitan Museum of Art, Cloisters Collection.

Large pitcher. Aileen O. Webb. The strong form and generous handle invite the viewer to pick it up and pour. Heavy reduction-fired stoneware. Courtesy of the artist.

Covered casserole. John Glick. Eight-quart capacity amply supported with sturdy handles. Courtesy of the artist.

Drinking mug. Polly Rothenberg. A gently curving top will accommodate the drinker's lower lip comfortably.

Pitcher. John Glick. Stoneware, reduction fired to cone 10. Ash and iron glaze. Holds 1½ quarts. 9″ high. Courtesy of the artist.

Dinner set. Mary Scheier. Stoneware. Glazed gray and brown. Handsome, functional, and impeccably crafted. Courtesy of the artist.

Pitcher. Miron Webster. Wheel-thrown stoneware, reduction fired to cone 10. Brushed stain and celadon glaze decoration. 7" high. Courtesy of the artist.

Covered jar. Miron Webster. Wheel-thrown stoneware. Pulled handle. Brushed stain and celadon glaze decoration. 8" high. Courtesy of the artist.

Decanter set. Harold Wesley Hunsicker. 17" high. Courtesy of the Butler Institute of American Art.

Hanging planters. Jack Feltman. The planter is first thrown as a bowl with extra clay in the bottom. The bowl is cut loose and turned upside down. *A half-inch hole is cut through the bottom,* dead center. *Then the bottom drainage spout is pulled up from excess clay. Semimat high magnesium white glaze with iron oxide decoration. The planters are fired only once. 15" high, 18" diameter. Courtesy of the artist.* Photo by Feltman.

Set of pitchers. Petr Svoboda. Czechoslovakia. Courtesy of the artist. Photo by Sirovy.

*Stoneware planter. Joan Martin. The base is slab
formed; the bowl is coiled. The slab pedestal is closed
at the bottom, open between bowl and base.
Vermiculite fills the hollow pedestal to catch and
hold moisture from the soil-filled bowl. Interior
is heavily glazed, exterior is unglazed and waxed.
Courtesy of the artist.*

Hanging lamp. Maurice Rothenberg. Built from slabs ½″ thick. Openings were cut and sides were joined when the clay was firm. Dark brown slip. 9″ high. Courtesy of the artist.

Coiled lantern. Heavily grogged brown stoneware, unglazed.

Wheel-thrown lantern. A casual pattern was freely cut out when the clay was firm. Unglazed with waxed exterior. Oxidized copper fittings. 10″ high, 8″ diameter.

SUN STORAGE POT. *Donald P. Taylor. Wheel-thrown and hand-built stoneware with sculptured decoration. Fired to cone 10. Clear glaze with Barnard slip to emphasize decoration. The cork is anchored with a brass chain and rings. This handsome storage jar is 9" high x 7" in diameter. Courtesy of the artist.* Photo by Donald P. Taylor.

Wine bottle. Thomas Shafer. Slab built, with wheel-thrown top. Reduction fired to cone 10. White glaze with brown, blue, and orange decoration. Courtesy of the artist.

NOSE POT. *Donald P. Taylor. Wheel-thrown and hand-built stoneware fired to cone 10. Clear glaze with Barnard slip decoration. 10½" high x 8" wide x 5½" diameter. Courtesy of the artist.* Photo by Donald P. Taylor.

Jug. Bob Richardson. Stoneware fired to cone 10 in a reduction atmosphere, with cone 019 luster decoration. Warm tan with gold, silver, and copper lusters. 12" high. Courtesy of the artist.

Covered jars. Maryrose Pilcher. Slab-formed and wheel-thrown stoneware, fired to cone 9 in reduction atmosphere. 2½' tall. Mrs. Pilcher teaches at Parkland College, Champaign, Illinois. Courtesy of the artist.

GREAT AMERICAN HIGHWAYS SERIES, III. *Bob Richardson. Stoneware covered jar. Reduction fired to cone 10. Unusual luster-covered handle treatment; lusters fired to cone 019. Mottled brown with gold, silver, and copper. Courtesy of the artist.*

LANDSCAPE SERIES, I (left) *and* III (right). *Bob Richardson. Stoneware covered jars. No. I: mottled brown glaze with red iron oxide top and bottom; copper luster handle and culvert; 20" high. No. III: warm white glaze with red iron oxide; gold, silver, and copper luster sunray handles; 16" high. Courtesy of the artist.*

*Covered jar. Thomas Sellers. Flat inset lid. Glazed
with semiopaque white brushed glaze. Fired to cone
04. 6" high. Courtesy of the artist.*

*Hexagonal bottles. Thomas Shafer. Slab built, with thrown tops. Reduction
fired to cone 10. White glaze with blue, brown, and orange decoration.
8" to 9" tall. Because of their shape, these decorative functional forms are easy
to store. Courtesy of the artist.*

Neatly stored unfired ceramic ware made by producing craftsman, Thomas Shafer. Photo by Shafer.

Julie Larson at the potter's wheel in the Larsons'
well-organized workshop. Photo by Bob Vigiletti.

Julie and Tyrone Larson with cat, Feldspar, in the
Larson showroom. Courtesy of the artist.

A tapestry of teapots. Jack Feltman, of California, throws spout, lid, and body for these handsome teapots directly off the mound. No trimming is necessary. Handles are pulled and applied as soon as the teapot is thrown. Although the teapots are similar, each has its own special character. The glaze is a high magnesium semimat white with iron oxide brushed decoration. Fired to cone 10. Photo by Feltman.

Pitchers, Jack Feltman. 10" to 12" high. High magnesium semimat white glaze
with iron oxide decoration. No two pitchers are exactly alike. Photo by Feltman.

Michael Frimkess of California with his Cretan vases. Each form is made from
25 pounds of clay. Courtesy of the artist.

NEW CERAMIC FORMS

Clay craftsmen are pulling off strong and audacious statements; a socially pertinent form may comment with force and at the same time be most suitable as a weed vase. New ceramics are sometimes serious, but often whimsical. Clay toys that move, forms combined with feathers, fur, or velvet, ceramic pillows just for "holding" are skillfully crafted and part of today's ceramic world. The forms pictured here are the creations of talented professional craftsmen. They are offered for your enjoyment and perhaps for your serious reflection.

GHETTO VOICE IN ORANGE. *Willis (Bing) Davis. Stoneware, wheel thrown and slab built, 10" x 5" x 5". Courtesy of the Columbus, Ohio, Gallery of Fine Arts, Afro-American Collection.*

GHETTO VOICES, VIII. *Willis (Bing) Davis. Low-fire clay, wheel thrown and slab formed, 18" x 12" x 12". Mr. Davis teaches at DePauw University, Greencastle, Indiana. Courtesy of the artist.*

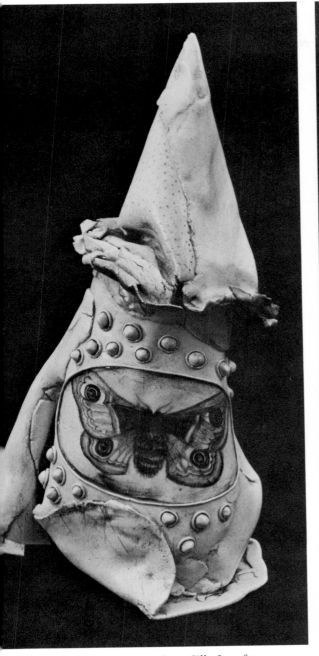

RELIQUARY FOR A MOTH. *Jesse Silk. Low-fire translucent body. Underglaze decoration. 9" high. Courtesy of the artist.*

RELIQUARY AND RELIGIOUS OBJECT. *Jesse Silk. Low-fire translucent clay body. Fishes and flower decoration in underglaze; top section with low-fire commercial glaze; midsection gold lustered, then rubbed off slightly. Courtesy of the artist.*

THE POTATO EATERS. *Linda Coghill. Earthenware lidded box with low-fire glazes. Outside of box lid is blue with gold stars. Interior of lid (not shown) is a collage of poverty scenes and parts of Van Gogh's painting* The Potato Eaters. *The box holding ceramic potatoes is red. Courtesy of the Utah Museum of Fine Arts, University of Utah, Salt Lake City.*

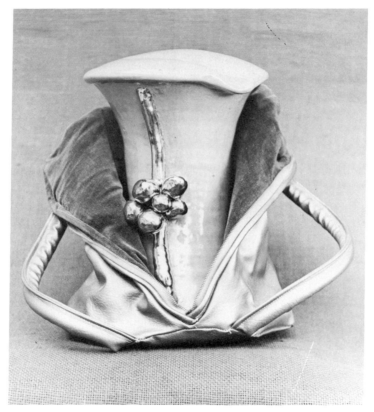

KANDY-KOATED TROPHY TO TIME, LIFE, AND
ACHIEVEMENT. *Randall Schmidt. One of a series.
Low-fire clay and glaze, gold luster, Naugahyde and
velvet, 16" high. Mr. Schmidt teaches at Arizona
State University at Tempe. Courtesy of the artist.*

DOGMAS. *Raul Coronel. Wheel-thrown stoneware, hand shaped. Dark brown with black slip wash. 24" high. From the Litton Collection, California.*

BIRD. *Donald P. Taylor. Wheel-thrown and hand-formed unglazed stoneware. Barnard slip decoration emphasizes modeling. Feathers attached. 5" in diameter. Courtesy of the artist.*

OLSTAD BLOWING HIS OWN HORN. *Don Olstad. Bright low-fire commercial glazes. Each part is 12 inches across. Courtesy of the artist.*

THE ULTIMATE IN APPLIED EYELASHES. *Justin Brady. Courtesy of the American Art Clay Company.*

CHROME CIRCUS. *Linda Coghill. Slip-cast earthenware with platinum luster overall. 32" high. Courtesy of the artist.*

Mechanical toys. Don Olstad. Courtesy of the artist.

Form for holding and feeling. Larry Calhoun. Ash glazed stoneware with cobalt decoration. Made of two slabs, 8 inches across. The form is hollow, supported on a velvet pillow. Mr. Calhoun teaches at the University of Akron, Ohio. Courtesy of the artist.

Form for holding. Larry Calhoun. Stoneware. Reduced iron stain. 8" wide, hollow. Courtesy of the artist.

*Vase forms. **Justin Brady**. Glazed designs over unglazed speckled stoneware.*
The animal form has a cornhusk tail. Courtesy of the American Art Clay Company.

JEWELRY FROM EGYPTIAN PASTE

Although ceramic clays such as stoneware and earthenware may seem to be a little heavy for wearing comfort when they are formed into jewelry, Egyptian paste is lightweight and beautifully self-glazing. This material is known traditionally as Egyptian faïence, but the name also identifies a tin-glazed majolica ware made in Faenza, Italy. In our time the material is known better as Egyptian *paste*. Developed in the remote fifth millennium B.C. as man's first glazed ware, Egyptian faïence has continued to be a favored material ever since then. It was made throughout the history of ancient Egyptian civilizations and later in the entire Mediterranean area. So great was the demand for faïence jewelry in ancient Egyptian courts that settlements of artisans sprang up within the confines of palace grounds and encompassing areas. Ruins of their "factories" reveal fragments of glaze crucibles, molds for jewelry, and miniature sculptures, with examples of the pieces in various stages of formation. These discoveries have been of help in reconstructing processes.

Egyptian paste is made in many colors, but by far the most popular ones have been the turquoises, blues, and greens that are developed with copper compounds. Other oxides are used to produce different colors: iron oxide for soft yellow, manganese oxide for purple, cobalt oxide for dark blue, and green from a mixture of copper and iron oxides. Because Egyptian paste has a low clay content and is not very plastic, it is most suited to miniature forms. It is a self-glazing body that can be made in the studio or bought commercially. A very satisfactory ready-prepared dry Egyptian paste in a variety of attractive colors can be purchased from studio suppliers. For those craftsmen who prefer to mix their own, the following recipe is offered:

BLUE EGYPTIAN PASTE

Feldspar (body)	40	grams
Flint	20	"
Fine white sand	8	"
Sodium bicarbonate (household quality)	6	"
Sodium carbonate	6	"
Calcium carbonate (whiting)	5	"
Bentonite	2	"
Copper carbonate	3	"
(Firing is to cone 012,) or 1600°F.		

The kiln heat should be watched carefully. Pieces will melt at too high temperature. The copper carbonate will make a deep rich blue. For light blue try 2 grams. Other oxide colorants are used in smaller amounts (about 1 gram).

Whether you use ready-prepared dry paste or mix your own, the dry ingredients should be blended thoroughly. Make a paste by adding water very gradually, a little at a time, kneading and blending it until it has the consistency of putty. (This is the point at which many novices have the most difficulty.) If it seems to crumble, add a very little water by just wetting your hands. Mix up just the amount you need for one working session.

When the paste is thoroughly blended, roll it into a thick coil and keep it wrapped in plastic as you pinch off small amounts and mold it into jewelry forms or diminutive sculptures. To make holes in beads, press the pointed end of a small watercolor brush handle into the bead lump. Rotate the brush handle gently so it does not force a crack when you press through the pellet from one side, then from the opposite side. If you dip the very tip end of the brush *handle* into water before you press it into the clay, it seems to slide through the form much easier. Avoid wetting it too much. As soon as each form is made, lay it gently on a nonabsorbent surface such as Formica for a few minutes, until it will hold its shape without sagging. When you have five or six beads formed, they must be prepared for drying.

As the Egyptian paste dries, soluble sodas in the mix drift or are drawn to the surface by capillary attraction, along with the moisture content, which evaporates and leaves a light sugary deposit called *efflorescence* on the surface of the forms. This deposit *forms the glaze* and it must not be disturbed or there will be no glazing action. Even when the beads seem dry, this efflorescence may continue to "bloom" on the surface. As soon as the beads will hold their form, they must be strung carefully on horizontal wires so that none are touching. Air will circulate around them while they dry, permitting an even accumulation of efflorescence over the surface of the small shapes. When all the jewelry segments are dry (this may take as long as two or more days), carefully restring them along clean short lengths of 14-gauge nichrome wire that has been coated with kiln wash solution; space them about ½ inch apart on the wires. Position small beads near the center of the wire, larger beads near the ends, so the wire does not sag in the middle. Wire ends are supported on sections of soft insulation brick, not firebrick, slotted with a saw to hold the wires. There are also a variety of bead-firing racks sold at ceramic supply shops. Support the racks high enough so that beads have plenty of clearance between them and the kiln shelf. Kiln wash on the wires will prevent them from sticking to the beads during firing. Fire to the recommended temperature, which may be from cone 08 to cone 010. If, in spite of your precautions, some of the beads should stick together when they are fired, pry them apart carefully when they have cooled. Some of them may break up and need replacing. It is wise to make more beads than you plan to use so you have plenty of spares.

When you begin the task of assembling the finished beads, spread them out and try several arrangements to see how they will look. At this point, you may decide to paint some of them with metallic or colored lusters. The pointed end of a small brush is excellent for holding each bead while you apply luster. Select the right-size brush handle so the bead does not slip down its length but remains impaled on the point while you paint it with luster. A pointed meat skewer is also useful for holding larger beads. Carefully transfer the painted bead to the nichrome wire of the firing rack (without touching the paint if possible!) by slipping it off the brush handle onto the wire end. Move each shape into place with the small brush you used for painting it, leaving ½ inch between each piece. Let the luster dry overnight in a warm place. The metallic fumes of the luster will be driven off slowly during the preliminary firing stage, so leave peepholes open for escaping gases; see that the room is well ventilated. Fire to cone 020, or to 1200°F.

Yarn or leather lacings are fine for stringing large beads and pendants. Nylon bead cord is available for small beads. Knots tied between a series of three to five beads are decorative and give flexibility to a necklace. Keep the beads smooth and small at the back of the neck for wearing comfort as well as for beauty.

The pointed tool is rotated gently so it does not force a crack as it is pressed through the pellet. Keep unused paste wrapped in plastic.

The handle of one brush anchors the two-holed bracelet segment while the other brush paints on the luster.

While the paste is drying, a light sugary deposit, called "efflorescence," is drawn to the surface. Because this deposit is the glaze, *it must not be disturbed.*

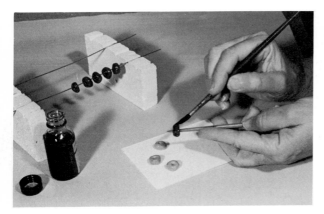

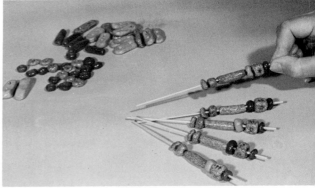

Impale the bead on a pointed stick while you brush it with colored luster. Avoid touching the luster paint after it is applied.

Beads for the tassel are lined up on a tiny dowel stick to see how they look. The beads have been painted with luster of matching color.

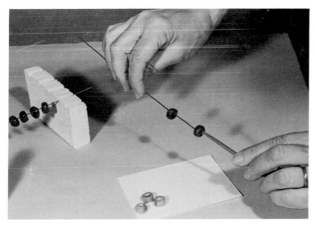

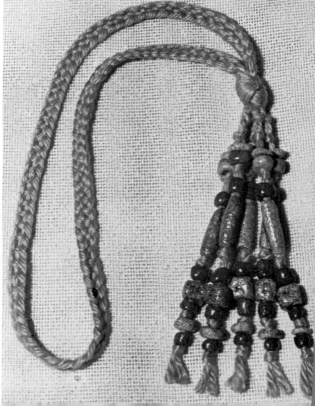

Carefully transfer the bead directly to the firing wire.

A woven gold yarn necklace with turquoise, blue, chartreuse, and green lustered bead tassel. Polly Rothenberg.

Egyptian-paste jerboas. These are replicas of tiny sculptures found in many tombs. The little animals have been inhabitants of African deserts since the second millennium B.C. *From the collection of Douglas Lowry, Fairborn, Ohio.*

Egyptian-paste necklaces. Douglas Lowry. The beads for the small necklace were molded on toothpicks. Courtesy of the artist.

Matching bracelet in turquoise and chartreuse.

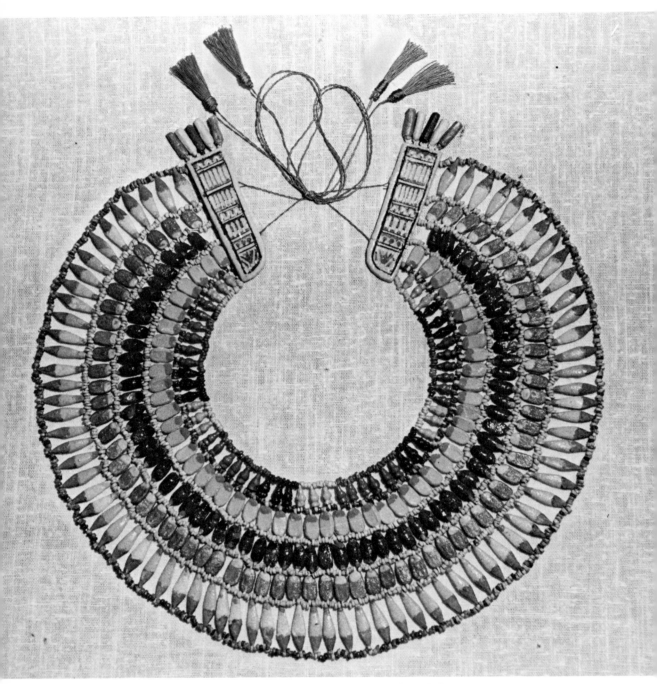

*Egyptian faïence collar. Douglas Lowry. Made of hundreds of hand-molded
beads in blues, greens, and pinks. Mr. Lowry has made a study of ancient
Egyptian art. Courtesy of the artist.*

BIBLIOGRAPHY

Anderson, Michael F. *Sculpture and Ideas.* Englewood Cliffs, N.J.: Prentice-Hall, Inc., 1966.

Ashton, Dore. *Modern American Sculpture.* New York: Harry N. Abrams, Inc., 1966.

Bager, Bertel. *Nature as Designer.* New York: Reinhold Publishing Corp., 1967.

Billington, Dora M. *The Technique of Pottery.* New York: Hearthside Press, Inc., 1962.

Binns, Charles F. *The Potter's Craft.* Princeton, N.J.: D. Van Nostrand Co., Inc., 1967.

Birren, Faber. *Creative Color.* New York: Reinhold Publishing Corp., 1961.

Clark, Kenneth. *Practical Pottery and Ceramics.* New York: The Viking Press, 1964.

Colbeck, John. *Pottery, the Technique of Throwing.* New York: Watson-Guptill Publications, and London: B. T. Batsford, Ltd., 1969.

Dawson, Robert. *Practical Sculpture.* New York: The Viking Press, and London: Studio Vista, Ltd., 1970.

DiValentin, Maria and Louis. *Sculpture for Beginners.* New York: Sterling Publishing Co., and London and Melbourne: The Oak Tree Press, 1965.

Ford, Betty Davenport. *Ceramic Sculpture.* New York: Reinhold Publishing Corp., 1964.

Gatz, Konrad. *Curtain Wall Construction.* New York: Frederick A. Praeger, 1965.

Gombrich, E. H. *The Story of Art.* Text edition. New York: Phaidon Publishers, Inc., 1966.

Green, David. *Pottery: Materials and Techniques.* New York: Frederick A. Praeger, 1967.

Hettes, Karel, and Pravoslav, Rada. *Modern Ceramics.* London: Spring Books, 1965.

Hofsted, Jolyon. *Step-by-Step Ceramics.* New York: Golden Press, 1967.

Isenstein, Harald. *Creative Clay Work.* New York: Sterling Publishing Co., Inc., 1960.

Johnson, Lillian. *Sculpture.* New York: David McKay Co., 1960.

Kenny, John B. *Ceramic Design.* New York: Pitman Publishing Corp., 1963.

————. *Ceramic Sculpture.* Philadelphia, New York, and London: Chilton Book Co., 1953.

————. *The Complete Book of Pottery Making.* New York: Greenberg, 1949.

Krum, Josephine. *Hand Built Pottery.* Scranton, Pa.: International Text Book Co., 1960.

Lundkvist, Lis and Hans. *Making Ceramics.* New York: Reinhold Publishing Corp., 1967.

Miller, Roy Andrew. *Japanese Ceramics.* Tokyo: Toto Shuppan Company, Ltd., 1960.

Nelson, Glenn C. *Ceramics: A Potter's Handbook.* New York: Holt, Rinehart, and Winston, 1966.

Petterson, Henry. *Creative Form in Clay.* New York: Reinhold Publishing Corp., 1968.

Piepenburg, Robert. *Raku Pottery.* The Macmillan Co., 1972.

Rhodes, Daniel. *Clays and Glazes for the Potter.* Philadelphia, Pa.: Chilton Book Co., 1957.

Röttger, Ernst. *Creative Clay Design.* New York: Reinhold Publishing Corp., 1963.

Schmitt-Menzel, Isolde. *Having Fun with Clay.* New York: Watson-Guptill Publications, 1968.

Sellers, Thomas. *Throwing on the Potter's Wheel.* Columbus, Ohio: Professional Publications, Inc., 1960.

Val Baker, Denys. *The Young Potter.* New York: Frederick Warne and Co., 1963.

Von Wuthenau, Alexander. *The Art of Terra-Cotta Pottery in Pre-Columbian, Central, and South America.* New York: Crown Publishers, Inc., 1970.

Willard, Paul. *A First Book of Ceramics.* New York: Funk and Wagnalls, 1969.

Winterburn, Mollie. *The Technique of Handbuilt Pottery.* New York: Watson-Guptill Publications, 1966.

Wright, Frank Lloyd. *An American Architecture.* New York: Horizon Press, 1955.

————. *The Natural House.* New York: Bramhall House, 1954.

PERIODICALS — *Ceramics Monthly,* Columbus, Ohio, *Craft Horizons,* New York City, *Design* magazine, Indianapolis, Ind.

GLOSSARY

(The glossary is intended for quick reference; consult index and text for detailed explanations. Definitions pertain particularly to ceramics.)

Absorption: The soaking up of water into porous material, such as clay or plaster.

Acid (in ceramics): Ingredients, such as silica and boric acid, which, when combined with metallic oxides, form a fusible glaze.

Air Bubbles: Pockets of air trapped in clay or plaster.

Albany Slip: A clay which, when used in its natural state, forms a charcoal brown glaze at cones 8 to 10; it is especially plentiful near Albany, New York.

Alkali: A soluble salt that lowers the melting point of glazes.

Alkaline Glaze: A nonlead frit glaze.

Alumina: Aluminum oxide (Al_2O_3), a highly refractory major metallic ingredient of clay. Used in glazes to retard running and to impart a mat finish.

Armature: A support around which clay is modeled; it may be of paper, wood, wire, plaster, or other material.

Ball Clay: A secondary clay of high plasticity and fine grain; it fires to white or cream color.

Ball Mill: Rotating porcelain cylinder containing small stones for grinding and blending clay bodies and glaze materials.

Banding Wheel: Portable turntable for rotating pottery while it is being formed, decorated, or otherwise worked on; also called a bench wheel.

Barium Carbonate: An extremely toxic substance to be avoided in most studios and *all* schools.

Basalt Ware: Clay made black by the addition of manganese, cobalt, or similar oxides to produce black basalt ware.

Bas-relief: Raised or carved patterns close to the plane of the surface.

Bat, Plaster: Slab on which pottery is formed or dried. It may be used to draw excess moisture from clay.

Batch: The ingredients of a glaze formula measured in proper portions for blending.

Beehive Kiln: Circular or cone-shaped kiln fired with wood, charcoal, or coke, tapered toward the top; of primitive origin.

Bench Wheel. See Banding Wheel.

Bentonite: Clay of volcanic ash origin used in small amounts to increase the plasticity of clay bodies; incorporated into glazes to aid uniform suspension of particles.

Binder: Natural or synthetic adhesive used to bind glazes to a ceramic object; burns out during firing. Also increases suspension of glaze particles in solution.

Biscuit. See Bisque.

Bisque: Ceramic ware that has been fired once without glaze.

Bisque Fire: First firing, without glaze.

Bisque Stains: Colorants painted or rubbed on fired ware or sculpture not intended to be refired.

Blisters: Bubbles formed during fast glaze firing by expanding air or steam unable to escape; usually avoided by slow steady firing.

Blowing: Pieces exploding in the kiln when being fired faster than the moisture content can escape; prevented by thorough drying and slow firing; also may be caused by residues of organic material that may be in the clay.

Blunger: A machine with rotating paddles for mixing slip or glazes.

Body Stains: Colorants added to plastic clay or slip.

Bone Ash: Calcined bones used to increase opacity of glazes and in production of bone china.

Bone Dry: Clay containing no absorbed moisture except air humidity: clay ready for firing.

Borax: A flux ingredient of low-firing glazes; preferred in calcined (dehydrated) form.

Boric Acid: An acid used in combination with metallic oxides in low fire glazes.

Bubbling: Eruption of gas, causing bubbles or pockmarks in glaze surfaces.

Burnishing: Polishing the surface of leather-hard clay by use of a smooth tool, stone, spoon back, or other smooth object.

Calcine: To drive out chemical water with slow heat, between $950°F.$ and $1300°F.$

Calcium Carbonate: An ingredient of chalk (whiting) used in high-firing glazes.

Calipers: A tool to measure diameter of objects.

Carbon Dioxide (CO_2): A gas produced by combustion when sufficient oxygen is present.

Carbon Monoxide (CO): A deadly gas produced by combustion when insufficient oxygen is present, often produced in reduction firing. Kiln rooms must be well ventilated; reduction kilns must have adequate flues.

Case: A mold used for casting other molds.

Casting: Pouring clay slip into plaster molds to produce copies of ceramic ware.

Chemical Water (chemically combined water): Water that is united in molecular combination with clay, as opposed to free water remaining in the pores between clay particles.

China Clay: High-fire white clay composed mostly of kaolin.

Chrome Oxide: Used in glazes to produce reds or greens.

Clay: Fine particles of decomposed granite or other feldspathic rock, becoming plastic when wet. Chemical formula is $Al_2O_3 \cdot 2\ SiO_2 \cdot 2\ H_2O$ in its pure state; but it usually contains impurities.

Clay Adhesive: Slurry containing a few drops of vinegar to promote adhesion in joining or repairing unfired clay.

Clay Body: A mixture of clays and other ceramic materials to achieve specific results in forming and firing.

Cobalt: A metallic source of blue colors.

Coiling: Using ropelike lengths of clay to build ceramic ware.

Colemanite (Gerstley Borate): A glaze ingredient used to lower the melting point.

Collaring: Reducing the diameter of the neck of a clay form, when throwing on the wheel, by pressing in with both hands.

Colloidal: A fluid consisting of fine particles remaining in suspension.

Cone, Pyrometric: A three-sided pyramid composed of clay and glaze factors made to bend and melt at specific temperatures; used to determine the end of firing or to shut off a kiln-sitter.

Copper Oxides: A source of black, blue green, and red colors.

Cracking: Splitting apart of a clay object while it is drying, firing, or cooling.

Crackle. See Crazing.

Crawling: Glaze running in folds, lumps, or patches during firing.

Crazing: Accidental or intentional crackling of glaze, usually caused by combining glazes that mature at different temperatures, or by glaze cooling faster than the body.

Crocus Martis: Purple red oxide of iron used to decorate bisque and to color glazes brown.

Dehydration: Loss of water by evaporation from plaster or clay.

Density: Weight related to volume.

Dipping: Immersing a clay object in glaze or engobe solution.

Dolomite: A mineral, calcium magnesium carbonate in crystal form; a fluxing agent in some glazes.

Drape Mold: Any form over which or into which a slab of clay is formed or draped to conform to the shape of the object.

Draping: Forming a clay object by placing a slab of clay over or into a preformed mold or other shape.

Dry-foot: To exclude or remove glaze from the bottom of a piece before it is fired.

Dunting: Fracturing of pieces in the kiln by uneven or fast cooling.

Earthenware: Porous pottery that matures at low-firing temperature.

Efflorescence: A bloom or powdery condition on a bisque surface caused by unneutralized soluble salts and sodas in the clay body, migrating to the surface of the body during drying.

Egyptian Paste: A low-fire self-glazing porous body, first developed in the fifth millennium B.C. by the Egyptians; it is used primarily for jewelry.

Embossing: Raised ornamentation.

Enamel: A vitreous composition applied by fusion to the surface of metal, glass, or pottery.

Engobe: White or colored clay slip used to decorate clayware before bisque firing.

Extruded Clay: Clay forced through an opening of a pug mill into a desired shape.

Faïence: Earthenware decorated with opaque colored glazes; also identifies Egyptian paste.

Fat Clay: Extremely plastic clay.

Feldspar: A rock that provides the principal components of most clay bodies.

Fettling: Trimming away unwanted clay seams or projections.

Filler: Nonplastic materials, such as grog or vermiculite, added to clay bodies to reduce shrinkage and hasten drying.

Filter Press: A device for removing excess water from clay by pressure.

Fire: To heat a clay object in a kiln to a specific temperature.

Firebox: Combustion chamber of a nonelectric fuel-burning kiln, below or adjacent to the firing chamber.

Firebrick: An insulation brick that withstands high temperatures in a kiln.

Firing Range: The span between the lowest and highest maturing temperatures of clay bodies or glazes.

Fit: Shrinkage during firing of glaze compatible with the shrinkage of a clay body it covers.

Flaking: Peeling off of glaze or slip.

Flint: A silica (SiO_2) material essential to ceramic clay.

Flocculate: To cause clay particles to aggregate into a mass.

Flocs: Thin, flat, oval crystals. Flocs cling closely together to form a compact mass.

Flue: The narrow area surrounding a fuel-burning kiln chamber through which the hot gases pass from the firebox, thus heating the kiln chamber.

Flux: Low melting components that combine easily with silica compounds to lower the fusing point of a clay body.

Foot: The base of a ceramic form.

Frit: Glaze that has been fired and reground to make its soluble materials insoluble, and to eliminate or reduce danger of chemical poisoning.

Fuse: To blend through heat by melting together.

Glaze: Glassy surface coating of vitreous material fired on ceramic ware to decorate it or to seal the pores.

Glaze Fit. See **Fit.**

Glaze Mist (Dust): Air pollutants from spraying or dusting glaze, harmful if inhaled; prevented by exhaust fans to carry it off.

Gloss Glaze: A shiny reflective glaze.

Granite: An igneous rock that decomposes into basic feldspathic clay ingredients.

Greenware: Unfired bone-dry ceramic objects.

Grog: Coarse, medium, or fine ground clay bisque added to a clay body to reduce warpage, shrinking, and cracking; also used to add texture to a clay surface.

Grout: Plaster, mortar, or similar compounds applied to fill spaces between tiles when they are mounted.

Gum. See **Binder.**

Gypsum: A hydrous calcium sulfate used in making plaster of Paris.

High Relief: A highly raised or deeply carved pattern on a clay surface.

Incising: Creating patterns by cutting on or through leather-hard clay.

Iron Oxide (Fe_2O_3): An ingredient of red clays. Also (FeO), a blue green colorant in reduction firing.

Jigger: A device on a turntable or wheel that trims off excess clay to form a predetermined shape.

Joggles: Domes and matching sockets for accurately aligning parts of a plaster mold.

Joining: Adhering clay surfaces together with cross-hatching, slurry, pressure, and tooling.

Junior Cones: Small pyrometric cones, especially useful in small kilns.

Kanthal: A metal alloy for producing elements in high-fire electric kilns, usually to 2300°F.

Kaolin ($Al_2O_3 \cdot 2\ SiO_2 \cdot 2\ H_2O$): Pure china clay, the principal ingredient for producing white porcelain ware; also an important ingredient in glazes.

Kiln: A furnace of refractory clay designed for firing ceramics and enamels, and for fusing glass.

Kiln Cement: A mixture of powdered fire clay and sodium silicate for mending kiln linings.

Kiln Elements: Nichrome or Kanthal wire heating coils, installed in the interior refractory surfaces of kilns.

Kiln Furniture: Refractory posts and shelves necessary for efficient stacking of ceramics in the kiln.

Kiln-guard: A backup safety device for electric cutoff of current at a predetermined time.

Kiln Plug: Solid small ceramic cylinders for plugging peepholes.

Kiln Posts: Ceramic posts designed to elevate and support kiln shelves during firing.

Kiln-sitter: An automatic device to shut off a kiln at the maximum temperature desired.

Kiln Wash: Equal parts of kaolin and flint in solution of water for coating kiln shelves and floors to protect them from glaze drippings.

Kneading: Manipulating plastic clay with the heel of the hand to achieve desirable consistency and to reduce air pockets.

Lead Glaze: A glaze containing raw lead, involving toxic hazards.

Lead Silicates: Glaze flux.

Leather Hard: Clay partly dried but still damp, firm, and easily carved.

Lime: Calcium carbonate used in glaze preparation.

Long: Fat or extremely plastic clay, caused by high percentage of moisture.

Luster (Lustre): A metallic iridescent glaze, low firing, usually cone 020 to 018.

Majolica: High gloss tin-bearing glaze.

Manganese: A chemical source of purple and brown glaze color.

Master Mold: A mold from which other molds are cast.

Mat (also Matt or Matte): A dull glaze surface with low reflectance when fired. It must have a slow cooling cycle or it may turn shiny.

Maturity: The temperature at which a clay body attains maximum hardness or at which a glaze fuses with a hard and attractive finish.

Mishima: Incised lines filled with engobe to the original level of surface.

Muffle: A kiln chamber to hold ceramic objects, around which the heat waves circulate.

Nickel Oxide: A glaze colorant; mostly greens and grays.

One-Step Firing: Glazed greenware fired once; not recommended.

Opacifiers: Specific oxides, such as tin, added to transparent glazes to make them opalescent or opaque.

Opaque Glaze: Nontransparent glaze that completely covers colors or clays under it. If lightly applied, clay color may come partly through.

Open Firing: Firing in a single chamber kiln where ceramic ware comes in contact with the flames.

Opening: The adding of grog to clay to increase porosity, reduce shrinkage, promote drying, and retard warpage.

Overglaze: The final glaze application of decorative details brushed over glaze; often a low-fire glaze over a prefired high-fire glaze.

Oxidation Fire: A kiln fired with a full supply of oxygen (as opposed to reduction firing); electric kilns are oxidation fired.

Oxides: Various metal compounds used as colorants in glazes and clay bodies.

Paste (Porcelain): A porcelain clay body made from kaolin, feldspar, and flint. See also **Egyptian Paste.**

Peeling: Glaze separation from a clay body because of incompatibility or careless handling.

Peephole: One or more openings through a kiln wall or door for viewing cones inside the kiln or to act as a vent for moisture release.

Petuntse: A partly decomposed feldspathic rock.

Pinch Pot: Finger manipulation of clay in the palm of the hand to form a lump of clay into a hollow shape.

Plaster Bat: A slab made of plaster.

Plaster of Paris: Powdered calcined gypsum which, when combined with water, sets up into an absorbent solid.

Plasticity: The quality of clay that allows it to maintain a shape attained by pressure deformation; capable of being molded.

Porcelain: A hard white translucent nonporous ceramic ware consisting mostly of kaolin, flint, and feldspar.

Porosity: The openness of a clay body; its ability to absorb and evaporate moisture, increased by the addition of grog.

Potash: An important glaze ingredient found in feldspar.

Pottery: Earthenware. Also a shop where ceramics are made.

Pouring (Casting) Mold: A hollow plaster form into which slip is poured to reproduce a clay shell replica of that particular form.

Pressing: To impress designs into clay with various plaster or other objects or carved stamps.

Primary (Residual) Clay: Clay found at the original rock site from which it was formed by decomposition.

Pug Mill: A machine for mixing clays and ingredients, reclaiming clay scraps, and preparing clay bodies to a uniform plastic consistency.

Pyrometer: A gauge that indicates kiln temperature; it supplements cones by indicating progressive changes during the firing cycle.

Quartz: Silican dioxide in crystalline structure.

Raku: A ceramic process using an open clay, heavy with grog. Highly resistant to sudden thermal changes; may be placed in and removed from a hot kiln. An ancient Oriental ceramic form associated with a ceremonial tea custom.

Raw Clay: Clay as it is mined from the ground, unblended with other clays and ceramic materials.

Raw Glazes (and **Glaze Components**): Consisting of nonfritted materials.

Reduction Firing: A firing in which there is insufficient oxygen available to consume the free carbon emanating from the heated glaze and clay, resulting in the formation of carbon monoxide. Oxygen-starved carbon monoxide pulls oxygen from the body and glaze, forming color changes in the coloring oxides.

Refractory: A hard heat-resisting nonmetallic ceramic material.

Residual Clay: Clay found at the original, or parent, rock site from which it was formed.

Rib: A rubber, metal, or wooden tool used to facilitate wheel-throwing of ceramic forms.

Rutile: Titanium dioxide containing iron or other impurity, giving a light tan or mottled effect.

Sagger (or **Saggar**): The chamber in a kiln holding ceramic pieces apart from the firing chamber, usually in a fuel-burning kiln.

Sagging: Slumping of plastic clay forms before the clay sets up.

Salt Glaze: A process of hard granular glazing resulting from throwing salt (NaCl) into a hot kiln.

Satin Glaze: A glaze with medium reflectance, between gloss and mat.

Scaling: A flaking or peeling of glazes.

Score: To scratch lines in unfired clay before applying moisture to facilitate joining; also to scratch decorative designs in unfired clay.

Sculpture: Modeling with plastic clay.

Secondary Clay: Plastic clay that has been transported from its original rock site and deposited elsewhere in layers.

Sedimentary Clay: The same as **Secondary Clay.**

Self-glazing Engobes: Engobes (or slip) containing a percentage of glaze materials to provide a gloss and a better seal.

Setting: The hardening of plaster after it is combined with water; also the firming of a clay body from loss of moisture.

Sgraffito: Decoration by incising or scratching through slip or glaze to reveal the background color or material.

Shard (Sherd): A broken piece of pottery.

Short: Stiff clay body caused by low moisture content: not very plastic.

Shrinkage: Contraction of clay by drying or firing.

Silica (SiO_2): Important glass-forming ingredient in glazes. An ingredient of kiln wash, clay, feldspar, quartz, and other ceramic materials.

Size (or **Sizing**): A solution, usually of soap, to prevent poured plaster from adhering to another plaster surface or other object.

Skive: To skim off in thin layers or pieces: to pare.

Slab Construction: Forms hand built with pressed or rolled flat sections of clay.

Slip: Liquid clay body, deflocculated when used for slip-casting.

Slip Trailer: A plastic squeeze bottle or device for extruding a thin trail of slip or engobe to make surface decoration.

Slumping. See Sagging.

Slurry: A clay body of a creamy consistency, used for joining moist clay sections.

Soaking: Maintaining a low steady heat in the initial stage of firing to achieve a uniform temperature throughout the kiln.

Stacking: Loading the kiln for maximum number of items with efficient distribution.

Stains. See Body Stains and Bisque Stains.

Stilts: Clay or metal-pointed refractory supports for elevating forms above the kiln floor or shelves.

Stoneware Clay: A high-temperature clay body that matures and fires to stoneware at cone 8, or higher, vitrifying at the higher temperatures to a nearly nonporous ware.

Tactile: Texture that can be felt by touching it.

Template: A pattern of paper, metal, or wood, placed against a clay surface or form, for guiding the shape of the design.

Terra Cotta: A popular grogged earthenware body of various yellow red hues used for sculpturing.

Throwing: Creating ceramic shapes on a potter's wheel.

Tin Oxide: White pigment used in glazes as an opacifier.

Titanium Dioxide (TiO_2): A cream or light buff colorant, used in glazes.

Toolmarks: Marks made by hands and forming tools that are left visible on a finished clay form as part of the completed design.

Trailing: The process of applying slip or glazes from a squeeze bottle to form an undulating or stringlike design.

Translucent: Transmits diffused light rays, as in porcelain or china, or in opalescent glazes.

Transparent: Transmits light rays with clear visibility.

Turning: Trimming on the potter's wheel when shapes are leather hard, usually to shape a wall, foot, or rim.

Undercut: A cut that slants inward, preventing a poured or cast form from being removed from a casting mold.

Underglaze: Any color application over which a glaze will be applied.

Uranium Oxide: A bright red colorant when it is fired low, turning to yellow when fired high.

Vinegar Additive: A few drops of vinegar added to slurry. Causes clay flocs to swell and increase bonding.

Vitrification: The firing stage at which the pores of a stoneware or porcelain clay body are filled with glassy silicates, mostly sealed against moisture.

Warping: Deformation of a clay shape caused by uneven stresses during shaping, drying, or firing.

Water Smoking: Evaporation of moisture from clay during early firing stages.

Wax Resist: Pattern created by brushing a wax medium over an area of clay, slip, or glaze to resist the final glaze application when the wax is dry.

Weathering: Exposing freshly dug clay to the weather for seasoning or breaking down particle size.

Wedging: Manipulating a clay body by twisting, kneading, or pounding to remove air pockets and develop a uniform plastic consistency.

Wheel: A rotating wheel for throwing technique; also a bench wheel or banding wheel for aid in hand-forming and decorating.

Whiting: Calcium carbonate, used frequently as a high-fire flux.

Zinc Oxide: An opaque white pigment used as a glaze colorant.

Zircopax: A glaze ingredient used to increase opacity.

SUPPLY SOURCES

UNITED STATES

Clays

American Art Clay Co.
4717 W. 16th Street
Indianapolis, Indiana 46222

House of Ceramics, Inc.
1011 N. Hollywood Street
Memphis, Tennessee 38108

Newton Pottery Supply Company
96 Rumford Avenue
Box 96
West Newton, Massachusetts 02165

Paramount Ceramics, Inc.
220 N. State
Fairmont, Minnesota 56031

Standard Ceramic Supply Co.
Box 4435
Pittsburgh, Pennsylvania 15205

Trinity Ceramic Supply, Inc.
9016 Diplomacy Row
Dallas, Texas 75235

Van Howe Ceramic Supply
11975 E. 40th
Denver, Colorado 80239

Glazes

American Art Clay Co.
4717 W. 16th Street
Indianapolis, Indiana 46222

Mayco Colors
20800 Dearborn Street
Chatsworth, California 91311

Reward Ceramic Color
    Manufacturers, Inc.
314 Hammonds Ferry Road
Glen Burnie
Maryland 21061

Richland Ceramics, Inc.
Box 3416
Columbia, South Carolina 29203

Standard Ceramic Supply Co.
Box 4435
Pittsburgh, Pennsylvania 15205

Tru-Fyre Ceramic Products Co.
5894 Blackwelder Street
Culver City, California 90230

Glaze Chemicals and Frits

Ceramic Color and Chemical Mfgr.
Box 297
New Brighton, Pennsylvania 15066

Creek-Turn Lab
Route 38
Hainesport, New Jersey 08036

Ferro Corporation
4150 E. 56th Street
Cleveland, Ohio 44105

Newton Potter's Supply, Inc.
96 Rumford Avenue
Box 96
West Newton, Massachusetts 02165

Pemco Corporation
5601 Eastern Avenue
Baltimore, Maryland 21202

Colored and Metallic Lusters

Standard Ceramic Supply Co.
Box 4435
Pittsburgh, Pennsylvania 15205

Pattern Paddles—
Custom Made

Chester Hollins
754 E. Dorothy Lane
Dayton, Ohio 45419

Raku Clays and Glazes

American Art Clay Co.
4717 W. 16th Street
Indianapolis, Indiana 46222

Raku Tongs—Extra Long

Robert Piepenburg
515 E. Windamere
Royal Oak, Michigan 48073

Tile Cement for Murals

Minnesota Mining and
    Manufacturing Co.

3-M Center
St. Paul, Minnesota 55119

Pug Mills

American Art Clay Co.
4717 W. 16th Street
Indianapolis, Indiana 46222

Walker-Jamar Co., Inc.
Duluth, Minnesota 55802

Equipment and Tools

Allcraft Tool and Supply Co.
215 Park Avenue
Hicksville, New York 11801

A. D. Alpine Co.
353 Coral Circle
El Segundo, California 90205

Cecas
Batavia Road
Warrenville, Illinois 60555

Kemper Manufacturing Co.
Box 545
Chino, California 91710

Skutt Ceramic Products
2618 S.E. Steele Street
Portland, Oregon 97202

Spraying Equipment

The Art Spray Co.
Box 4577
Walnut Creek, California 94956

Kilns

A-1 Kiln Manufacturers
Box 1014
Felton, California 95018

Aim Ceramic Kilns
Hiway 9 and Brookside
Box 414 C
Ben Lomond, California 94930

American Art Clay Co.
4717 W. 16th Street
Indianapolis, Indiana 46222

W. D. Burt Mfg. Co.
Box 353
Fairfax, California 94930

J. J. Cress Co., Inc.
1718 Floradale Avenue
South El Monte, California 91733

Jay-Bellman
1051 N. Edgemont
La Habra, California 90631

L&L Manufacturing Co.
144 Conchester Road
Twin Oaks, Pennsylvania 19104

Skutt Ceramic Products
2618 S.E. Steele Street
Portland, Oregon 97202

Unique Kilns Division
H E D Industries, Inc.
Box 176
Pennington, New Jersey 08534

Westby Ceramic Supply & Mfg. Co.
408 N.E. 72nd Street
Seattle, Washington 98115

Potter's Wheels

The A-J Co.
Box 31
Quitman, Georgia 31643

American Art Clay Co.
4717 W. 16th Street
Indianapolis, Indiana 46222

B and I Manufacturing Co.
Burlington, Wisconsin 53105

Harve Bergman
15477 Moorpark #3
Sherman Oaks, California 91403

Robert Brent Potter's Wheels
1101 Cedar Street
Santa Monica, California 90405

Gilmour Campbell
14258 Maiden
Detroit, Michigan 48213

H. B. Klopfenstein & Sons
R.F.D. 2
Crestline, Ohio 44827

LTM Corporation
855 S. Telegraph Road
Monroe, Michigan 48167

Oscar-Paul Corporation
522 W. 182nd Street
Gardena, California 90247

Pacifica Potter's Wheels
Box 924
Berkeley, California 94701

Parfex Co.
7812 Boulder Avenue
Highland, California 92346

Shimpo-West
Box 2315
La Puente, California 91746

Ceramic Supplies—General

Alaska Mud Puddle
9034 Hartzell Road
Anchorage, Alaska 99502

Bergen Arts and Crafts
Box 689
Salem, Massachusetts 01971

Bovin Ceramics
6912 Schaeffer Road
Dearborn, Michigan 48126

Capital Ceramics
2174 S. Main Street
Salt Lake City, Utah 84115

Central New York Ceramic Supply
213–215 Second Street
Liverpool, New York 13088

Ceramics, Hawaii Ltd.
629 Cooke Street
Honolulu, Hawaii 96813

Creek-Turn Lab
Route 38
Hainesport, New Jersey 08036

Cross Creek Ceramics
3596 Brownsville Road
Pittsburgh, Pennsylvania 15227

C. R. Hill Company
35 West Grand River
Detroit, Michigan 48226

Newton Potter's Supply, Inc.
96 Rumford Avenue
Box 96
West Newton, Massachusetts 02165

Ohio Ceramic Supply, Inc.
Box 630
Kent, Ohio 44240

Paramount Ceramics, Inc.
220 N. State
Fairmont, Minnesota 56031

Richland Ceramics, Inc.
Box 3416
Columbia, South Carolina 29203

Sax Arts and Crafts
207 N. Milwaukee Street
Milwaukee, Wisconsin 53202

Standard Ceramic Supply Co.
Box 4435
Pittsburgh, Pennsylvania 15205

Tepping Studio Supply Co.
3003 Salem Avenue
Dayton, Ohio 45406

Terra Ceramics
3035 Koapako Street
Honolulu, Hawaii 96819

Trinity Ceramic Supply, Inc.
9016 Diplomacy Row
Dallas, Texas 75235

Van Howe Ceramic Supply Co.
4216 Edith N.E.
Albuquerque, New Mexico 87107

Western Ceramics Supply Co.
1601 Howard Street
San Francisco, California 94103

Westwood Ceramics Supply Co.
14400 Lomitas Avenue
City of Industry, California 91744

ENGLAND

Clays

English China Clay Ltd.
18 High Cross Street
St. Austell, Cornwall

Pike Brothers
Wareham, Dorset

Potclays Ltd.
Wharf House
Copeland Street
Hanley, Stoke-on-Trent

Watts Blake and Bearn Ltd.
Newton Abbot, Devon

Glazes and Components

Blythe Color Works Ltd.
Cresswell, Stoke-on-Trent

E. W. Good & Co. Ltd.
Barker Street
Longton, Stoke-on-Trent

George Goodwin & Son Ltd.
Westwood Mills, Lichfield Street
Hanley, Stoke-on-Trent

Reeves & Sons Ltd.
Enfield, Middlesex

Wengers Ltd.
Etruria, Stoke-on-Trent

Kilns

Applied Heat Co. Ltd.
Elecfurn Works, Otterspool Way
Watford-by-Pass
Watford, Hertfordshire

British Ceramic Service Co. Ltd.
Park Avenue
Wolstanton, Newcastle, Staffordshire

Cromartie Kilns
Dividy Road
Longton, Staffordshire

Dawson-Mason Gas Plant Co. Ltd.
Alma Works
Levenshulme, Manchester 19

Kilns and Furnaces Ltd.
Keele Street Works
Tunstall, Stoke-on-Trent

Bernard W. E. Webber Ltd.
Alfred Street
Fenton, Stoke-on-Trent

Ceramic Supplies and Equipment

Fulham Pottery Ltd.
210 New Kings Road
London SW6

W. Podmore & Sons Ltd.
Caledonian Mills
Shelton, Stoke-on-Trent

Potter's Equipment Co.
73–77 Britannia Road
London SW6

Wengers Ltd.
Etruria, Stoke-on-Trent

Throwing Bats, Asbestos

Bingley, Son & Follit Ltd.
Millbank Works
Minerva Road, London NW10

Potter's Wheels

Associated Pump Ltd.
73 Britannia Road
London SW6

W. Boulton & Co.
Burslem, Stoke-on-Trent

Corbic
Gomshall, Surrey

Judson and Hudson Ltd.
Keighley, Yorkshire

The Leach Pottery
St. Ives, Cornwall

Alec Tiranti
72 Charlotte Street
London W1

Bernard W. E. Webber Ltd.
Alfred Street
Fenton, Stoke-on-Trent

CANADA

Clays

Baroid of Canada Ltd.
5108 Eighth Avenue SW
Calgary, Alberta

Jean Cartier
1029 Bleury Street
Montreal, P.Q.

Clayburn Harbison Ltd.
1690 West Broadway
Vancouver, British Columbia

A. P. Green Firebrick Co.
Rosemont Avenue
Weston, Ontario

Magobac Mining Co.
510 Fifth Street SW
Calgary, Alberta

Pembena Mountain Clay
945 Logan
Winnipeg, Manitoba

Saskatchewan Clay Products
Box 970
Estevan, Saskatchewan

Glazes and Components

Barrett Company Ltd.
1155 Dorchester Blvd., W
Montreal 2, P.Q.

Blythe Colors Ltd.
Toronto, Ontario

E. Harris & Co., of Toronto Ltd.
73 King Street
East Toronto, Ontario

Ceramic Supplies
and Equipment

Advance Ceramics
820 Renfree Street
Vancouver 6, British Columbia

Alberta Ceramic Supplies
8520 67th Avenue
Edmonton, Alberta

Ceramicraft Ltd.
594 Notre Dame Avenue
Winnipeg 2, Manitoba

Coast Ceramics Ltd.
3739 West 16th
Vancouver, British Columbia

Cobequid Ceramics
102 Smith Avenue
Truro, Nova Scotia

Greater Toronto Ceramic Center
167 Lakeshore Road
Toronto 14, Ontario

Mercedes Ceramic Supply
8 Wallace Street
Woodbridge, Ontario

Pottery Supply House
491 Wildwood Road
Oakville, Ontario

Regina Ceramic Co.
1605 10th Avenue
Regina, Saskatchewan

Universal Ceramics
623 8th Avenue SW
Calgary 2, Alberta

Village Ceramic Studio
4949 Dundas Street
West Islington, Ontario

Potter's Wheels and Kilns

Hurley Bennett
1497 Pierre Avenue
Windsor, Ontario

Estrin Manufacturing Ltd.
3651 Pt. Grey Road
Vancouver, British Columbia

C. W. Ride
North Hatley, P.Q.

W. H. Williams
144 Westwood Avenue
Hamilton, Ontario

Kilns

Hurley Bennett
1497 Pierre Avenue
Windsor, Ontario

INDEX

A

Adhesive, 13, 220
Aging clay, 9
Air pockets (bubbles)
  clay, 10
  plaster, 15, 17
Alumina, 2, 111
Aluminum silicate, 2
American Art Clay Co., 12, 63, 64, 112, 199, 255, 257
Appliqué, clay, 107, 128, 129, 131, 140, 141
Architectural ceramics, 209–18
Arend, Lucien den, 229–32
Armatures, 190–93

B

Ball clay, 4, 5
Banding wheel (bench wheel), 37, 47–49, 51–57, 62, 68, 75, 144, 162, 190–92, 211
Barlow, Helen, 200
Bats, plaster (see plaster bats)
Bauer, Patti Warashina, 10
Bench wheel (see banding wheel)
Bentonite, 4, 5
Bibliography, 263
Bisque (bisquit), 110–12, 159, 264
Black, David, 155, 156
Bogatay, Paul, 187
Bone dry, 15, 183, 264
Bottles, thrown, 95–97
Bouman, Jacques, 217
Bowls, thrown, 91–93
Box construction, 25, 26, 34, 35, 172, 173
Brady, Justin, 255, 257
Brosz, Victor, 179
Brushing glazes, 158–60
Bubbles,
  in clay, 10
  in plaster, 15, 17
Burnishing clay, 41, 56
Buthaud, René, XII, facing page 1
Butler Institute of American Art, 4, 29, 59, 73, 116, 125, 130, 143, 155, 156, 186, 187, 237
Buying clay, 6

C

Calhoun, Larry, 146, 153, 256
Calipers, 101
Candle holders, clay, 30–33
Carbonaceous materials, 4

Carved designs, 124, 125
Casting mold, 72, 76, 80–84
  altering the cast form, 83
Centering clay, 85–89, 91, 102
Ceramic design and decoration, 113–67
Ceramics Monthly magazine, 44, 45, 120, 121, 143, 182, 218, 263
Characteristics of clay, 2, 3, 10
China clay, 3, 5, 6
Chinese tomb figure, 198
Chuck for foot rimming, 104
Clay, 2–14
  aging of, 9
  Bentonite, 4
  bodies, 2, 4–6, 85
  ceramic, 2, 4–6
  characteristics of, 2, 3, 10
  chemical formula, 2
  clogging of drains, 14
  colors of, 2
  common, 3
  compacting, 108, 182, 195
  composition of, 2–6
  deflocculate, 80
  dry, 6, 8
  drying and shrinkage, 3–5, 14, 15
  earthenware, 3, 4
  fire clay, 4
  firing of, 15, 108, 111, 112, 183
  flocs, 10, 80
  flour, 6, 8
  formation of, 2
  fundamentals, 10
  joining, 13, 29
  kneading, 11, 185
  mixing, 6, 8–10, 12, 13
  modeling clay, 5
  natural, 2, 3
  nature of, 1, 2
  origin, 2
  particles (flocs), 2, 3, 10, 80
  plasticity of, 1, 10
  porosity of, 2–5, 14
  preparation, 6
  primary, 2
  residual, 2
  reworking, 11–13
  sculpture clay, 5, 168, 169
  secondary, 2
  sedimentary, 2
  selecting, 6
  shrinkage of, 3–5, 10
  slip, 14, 128
  slurry, 13

  stoneware, 3, 5
  storing, 6, 8, 9
  throwing clay bodies, 5, 85
  weathering of, 2
  wedging, 10, 11
Clay bodies, earthenware, 4
  porcelain, 5
  sculpture bodies, 5
  selecting, 6
  stoneware, 5
  wheel throwing bodies, 5, 85
Cloisonné, clay, 132, 133
Coghill, Linda, 252, 255
Coil construction, 50–64
  sculpture, 195–98, 214
  wall, 212, 213
Compacting clay, 182, 195
Cone, pyrometric, 108–12
  temperature equivalent chart, 109
Cooper-Hewitt Museum, 7, 76, 152
Coronel, Raul, 3, 21, 90, 169, 171, 179, 188, 189, 200, 201, 209–11, 253
Craft Horizons, 263
Cross Creek Ceramics, 82–84

D

Damp box, 15, 19
Damp cupboard, 15
Davis, Willis (Bing), 250
Decorating on the wheel, 149
Decorating with slip, 144–49
Decoration, 113–67
  appliqué, 128–37
  glazing, 157–62
  inlay, 138–41
  with lump enamel, 165–67
  lusters, 163–65
  slip techniques, 144–49
  sources for, 114
  texturing and impressing, 118–27
  tooling, 62, 129, 136, 137, 143
  wax resist and oxides, 155, 156
Deflocculant, 10, 80
Den Arend, Lucien, 229–32
Design (see Decoration)
Design magazine, 128, 209, 263
Dipping glazes, 160, 162
Dipping tongs, 160
Dlugosz, Louis, 63, 64
Drains clogged by clay, 14
Drape molds, 65–67
Drying clay, 14, 15
Dunn, Laura, 83, 84

E

Earthenware, 3, 4
Egyptian paste (Faïence), 258–62
  firing, 258, 259
  formula, 258
  glazing action, 259, 260
  history of, 258
  mixing, 258
Eisner, Vivienne, 202
Enamel decoration, 75, 165–67
Engobes (slip), 144–49
  decorating on the wheel, 149
  painting, 31, 32, 63, 129, 155
  trailing, 148

F

Faïence (Egyptian paste), 258–62
Feldspar, 2, 220, 258
Feltman, Jack, 27, 103, 105, 157, 238, 248, 249
Finger-pinched shapes, 22–27
Fire clay, 4, 5
Firing schedule, 111, 112, 183
  for sculpture, 183
Firing the kiln, 108–12, 183
  preparation, 108
  raku, 220–24
Flanged bowl with lid, 99–101
Flocs, 10, 80
Flocculate, 10, 80
Foot rims, 25, 103, 104, 166
Fountain, ceramic, 209
Frimkess, Michael, 249
Functional ware, 233–49
Fundamentals, 10
Funk, Verne, 121

G

Geometric sculpture, 171–77
Glaze handling,
  safety measures, 157–60
Glaze mixing and application, 157–62
  sculpture, 183
  raku, 220–21
Glazing, 157–63
  brushing, 158–60
  dipping, 160–62
  for raku, 220–21
  pouring, 159
  spraying, 162, 163
Glick, John, 235
Glick, Ruby, 58
Glossary, 264–69
Goslee, M. E., 125
Graup, Pauline, 83
Greenware, 80, 83, 84, 159
Grimm, Raymond, 13, 20, 117, 181, 215, 233

Grog
  artistic qualities, 14
  colors, 14
  fusing temperature, 14
  screening of, 14
  shrinkage deterrent, 14
  texturing qualities, 14, 126
Grossman, Maurice, 5, 106, 107

H

Handles, 98, 99, 104, 105, 233
Hay, Dick, 73
Hickey, Mary, 83
Hispano-Moresque, 46–50
Homogenous clay, 11
Hotchkiss, Dorothy Larson, 152
Hunsicker, Harold Wesley, 237

I

Impressing, 118–23, 126, 127
Incising, 41, 62, 124, 130, 134, 136, 137, 143
Inlay, clay, 138–41
  cut, 140, 141
  rolled, 138, 139
Intaglio,
  stamps, 119
  tiles, 73
Iron compounds, 2, 4, 5, 43

J

Jewelry, 258–62
Joining (jointing) of clay, 13, 29

K

Kaolin, 3, 5
Kidney
  rubber, 27, 54, 65, 81, 94, 173, 195
  wood, 89
Kiln
  firing, 108–12
  furniture, 110
  shelves, 110
  stacking, 110–12
  wash, 110
Kiln, Tom Shafer's, 50
Kiln, Robert Piepenburg's raku, 222
Kleek, Anne van, 130
Kneading clay, 11, 185
Kristensen, Gail, 26, 36, 42–44, 54, 59, 125, 151, 152, 158, 172, 215
Kuch, Elly, 4, 20, 114, 203

L

Lakofsky, Charles, 186
Lamps and lanterns, 59–63, 211, 240
Larson, Julie, 53, 97, 164, 247
Larson, Tyrone, 97, 98, 247

Leather hard, 15
Lifter, clay, 87, 97
Linoleum cuts,
  as press molds, 127
Lowry, Douglas, 261, 262
Lump enamel,
  for decorating, 165–67
Lusters, 7, 10, 97, 98, 163–65
  application of, 163, 164
  firing, 163, 164

M

McCormick, Patrick, 164, 165, 204, 205
McVey, Leza, 116
Maher, Lois, 199
Malinowski, Arno, 7
Manganese dioxide, 43, 44
Martin, Joan, 127, 239
Mateescu, Patriciu, 167, 170, 188
Metropolitan Museum of Art, facing page 1, 198, 233
Miles Laboratory, 210, 211
Mishima, 147, 148
Modeling and sculpturing tools, 184, 191, 192, 195
Mold casting, 80–84
  altering the cast form, 83
Molds
  casting, 72, 80–84
  drape, 62, 63, 65–67, 74–76
  lino-cut, 127
  improvised, 65, 74–76
  making, 65–67, 69–79
  press, 48, 70–73, 119–23, 127
Mookhoek, Cees, 216–18
Muenger, Barbara, 59
Mullite, 111
Murals, 142, 209–18

N

Nakamura, Kimpei, 120, 143
New ceramic forms, 250–57

O

Olstad, Don, 77, 78, 254, 255
Open coil construction, 58–64
Orton, Edward Jr., Foundation, 109
Oxide colorants, 8, 43, 59, 119, 142, 150–56, 172, 220
Oxides, 2, 119, 153, 154

P

Paddles, texture, 126, 127
  pattern, 126, 127
Paddling, 47–49, 126, 127, 183, 196
Panels, 58, 70–73, 128, 129, 132–35, 147, 148, 215